C

Pro

T

NCC Blackwell

M A N C H E S T E R • O X F O R D

British Library Cataloguing in Publication Data
Blacklock, Phil

Computer programming. — 3rd ed.
Computer systems. Programming
I. Title II. Chantler, Alan. Programming techniques and practice
005.1

ISBN 1-85554-206-4

First published in 1981 as *Programming Techniques and Practice* by
Alan Chantler, reprinted 1987.

This fully revised and updated edition published in 1992 by:
NCC Blackwell Limited, 108 Cowley Road, Oxford OX4 1JF, England.

Editorial office: The National Computing Centre Limited,
Oxford House, Oxford Road, Manchester M1 7ED, England.

Typeset in Palatino/Futura by Wordshop, St Dennis

Printed In Singapore By Chong Moh Offset Printing Pte. Ltd.

Acknowledgements

Thanks must go to my father, without whom none of this would have been possible.

I would also like to thank the editors at NCC Blackwell for their help in producing this book.

Preface

Read me

I hope you enjoy reading and working with this book as much as we enjoyed producing it. To make that possible, read this introduction quickly; it includes details about how to use the book, and points to save you time and trouble.

Information technology (IT), the broad field of which computing is a crucial part, is very important as the basis of many aspects of modern life. It's an exciting subject to explore – not just for that reason, but because it's changing very fast: it's an area in which science fiction very quickly turns into fact. Every week, there are new developments; many of these are likely to affect the lives of most people in a short time.

People often think that IT and computing involves no more than the hardware – the equipment you use that you can touch. No so – much more important is software, the instructions in some kind of form that tells the hardware what to do from moment to moment, and how to do it. A significant part of the task of producing software is programming – writing good programs, which are sets of instructions designed to carry out given tasks for the user.

There are more jobs around in programming, software design, and software engineering than in hardware design. Work with software offers at least as much challenge as work with hardware, and it can often be a lot more interesting.

I mentioned above the problem of the rapid rate of change in IT; that's just as true of the software field as of hardware. Every year, important new types of program appear as people explore new uses of IT. Every year, too, whole new approaches to software design become important.

All the same, I believe this book adequately covers your needs. I've used all available information on NCC's Threshold and Diploma syllabuses to prepare it, and on other relevant introductory programming courses in various countries. I include various methods of helping you study further. (I'll come back to those shortly.)

Mind you, this is not *quite* an introductory text. Before you start on it, you need some basic concepts and skills, to:

 – know what a program is

- understand that a modern high level program language (such as Basic) consists of a small set of key words and a fairly small set of rules (syntax) for their use

- have done some high level computer programming, in, perhaps, Basic, dBase or Logo

- appreciate that programming involves the stages of

> careful planning of the program's specification
>
> the program itself (coding)
>
> thorough testing to ensure the program works properly
>
> documentation – providing notes on the code and clear friendly instructions for users

- understand the nature of pseudocode.

If any or all of that is new to you, that doesn't mean this book is useless – but it *does* mean you will have to work harder on it.

On the other hand, this is not a text that will help you to program in any specific language either. Here we deal with concepts, and study examples in pseudocode. Of course, I mention some major program languages in passing, and look at how to compare them – but we assume you will carry out your practical programming under other guidance than this book. After all, there are hundreds of program languages, and many of them have dozens of versions (dialects).

This book's too fat

All the same, for two reasons there's more in this book than you may need for your particular course. First, each course includes some topics others omit, so there's material here you don't need but others do. Secondly, I've tried to look forward, so I include a few aspects no exam board yet asks for.

All the same, as I say, the book's very closely linked to the needs of the *Programming techniques and practice* modules of the NCC's international Threshold and Diploma courses. If you are working on one of those, you will need to understand almost everything.

Otherwise, there are three ways you can find out what you need to study and what you can skip. The first is to rely on your teachers to tell you: you can assume that they have carried out the research needed to know your syllabus in detail.

The second is for you to study the syllabus. However, syllabuses are often rather vague, and reading yours may not help you as much as you would like. In fact, exam boards provide syllabuses for the teachers – who know what all the terms mean and have a feeling for required level of detail – rather than for the learners.

The third approach is to look at, and to try working with, actual exam papers. In this book, with many thanks to the sources for permission, I include a number of "real" questions.

However you go about that research, you may perhaps find areas in your course not treated in this book. That's because some boards offer choice between areas covered in great depth. You may need supplementary reading in that case – if you have a teacher, ask what other books you can use.

The exam boards vary, too, in their methods of assessing students. You may, or may not, have some kind of case study (program project) to explore; if you do, the amount of work will depend on the board.

Working with exam questions

Here's how best to use a "real" exam question like the ones I supply.

Read quickly through it, then do as much work as you think you need to be able to write a good answer. That work may include study of your notes, this book and other books; talk with fellow students on the course, your teachers, and others; thought; planning.

Then leave the question, for as much as a day if you can. When you come to attempt it for real, do so under exam conditions – with no help, no music, no interruptions, and in the correct time for the question. (Take the time to be at the rate of a couple of minutes per mark, unless you've found out otherwise.) Only then, look at the notes at the end of the book.

MORE questions?

There's another source of useful questions in this book. Near the start of each chapter I've put a list of objectives; the list begins "When you have worked through this chapter, you should be able to . . .". In effect, I've written each objective in the list in the form of a question you can set yourself as a quick revision test.

That's not the real reason I've put in those lists of objectives, though. They are, perhaps, the best way for you to relate this book to your syllabus and to your progress through the course.

Note: For the sake of brevity and easy reading the masculine pronoun "he" has been used whenever the "he/she" option was meant. This is not intended to suggest masculine superiority in any way, but has been used merely as a convenience.

Contents

Appendix

1   What is a program?

OBJECTIVES

When you have worked through this chapter, you should be able to:

- explain what a statement is
- state the nature of assignment, with examples
- explain, with examples, how simple and compound statements differ
- list the standard arithmetic and logical operators
- explain the nature of loops, and the difference between REPEAT and WHILE loops
- explain the nature of conditional branching, and the difference between simple, compound, and alternate IF sequences and the CASE structure
- state the nature of procedures (closed sub-routines), parameter-passing and global and local data.

INTRODUCTION

A program consists of a sequence of statements (instructions) in order to carry out a defined task.

In this chapter we look at some basic types of statement, some operators, some major key words for data input and output, and the most significant types of program structue. I use pseudocode throughout, rather than any specific program language. That means we can concentrate on principles rather than worrying about details that apply to only some cases.

On the other hand, you may be using a program language which doesn't offer all the key words, operators or structures we discuss. No matter – they are *all* important in theory; also you need to understand them, so you can try to use the features of the language you have, to model those you do not have.

So – what about those structures? Almost all so called linear programs are of little value; by linear program, I mean one that starts at the beginning and goes through in a straight line to the end. That may sound very efficient: in fact, in practice it is not likely to be efficient. The reason is that the power of an IT system involves what we call branching – taking different paths between start and end as circumstances require.

The simplest branching structure is:

IF such and such THEN do this

When the program reaches this point it will either "do this" or not.

In this chapter, we shall meet more sophisticated ways to control program branching, including two types of loop.

The final aspect of program structure we mention here is the procedure, or sub-routine. Again, only the simplest programs can manage without using this technique.

1.1 DATA HANDLING

The main function of a computer program is to process data. In other words, the program:

- accepts data from outside the computer as its input
- carries out a set of processes on the data
- stores the data for future use, and
- presents the results of this processing as its output.

In a given case, the input may be the details of an order from a client, with an invoice as output; or the input may be the temperature in an automatic washing machine, the output being an instruction to change the washing cycle.

Whatever may be the task of a computer program, that task requires "data". What is this data? It relates to what people call information, something that adds to human knowledge. Information means something to people, but computers have no intelligence so information has no meaning to them. Data is information inside an information technology (IT) system, such as a computer. Information may exist in many forms – such as handwritten documents, printed forms, the pressure in a gas; data has many forms too – for instance, coded magnetic tapes, voltages in the circuit of a chip, signals in a phone line. In the context of a computer program, data is a sequence of 0's and 1's, that stand, in coded form, for the information handled by the system. We'll deal with this more fully in the next chapter.

Data declaration

There are very many different "program languages", sets of rules and special (key) words people use to give instructions to an IT system. Almost all program languages expect the program to start by declaring any data items used by it. This means listing the name given to each item of data (we call the name a label or identifier), and stating what kind of data it is (for instance, a number or letter of the alphabet). Then, when the special translating program (a "compiler", for instance) turns our instructions into a form the system can use, it can give the correct interpretation to each label. That will ensure the program treats a number as a number and not as a character, for instance.

Examples of such declarations are:

INTEGER page-number; REAL distance; STRING message-text;

This tells the compiler that, for instance, page-number is a label (or name) for a data item the system should treat as an integer (whole number). We call the data items known by labels variables – their values may change during a run of the program.

Some data of course does not change. We can declare it as a constant (a "read only" variable) as in

page-length 66; pi 3.14159; message-text "Please try again";

In the case of some program languages, declaring variables and constants also reserves the right amount of main storage space; with other languages, you must first define data items to reserve storage and then declare them before use.

1.2 PSEUDOCODE IN USE

A computer uses 0s and 1s not only for data values, but to code its instructions. This so called machine code is not easy for people to understand and use – a programmer finds the task of communicating with the system much more straight forward when using a program language such as COBOL or Ada. These higher level languages have structures that are more natural for people to work with; they often use English-like words, as we have seen. The translation program puts these into the corresponding machine code form. For instance:

COBOL	Machine Code
ADD bill TO tax GIVING total	00100 0000000111
Ada	
total := bill + tax ;	10000 0000001001

These examples show the same process – that of simple addition. Which form is easier to understand? Notice the very different ways in which Ada and COBOL assign the sum of bill and tax to the label total. One uses the key word GIVING; the other the symbol := – and the structure (or syntax) differs too. Sometimes COBOL also uses the symbol =, for instance in the COMPUTE statement.

This is a very simple example of the confusion which can arise when we try to work with computer program languages. A common solution to the problem is to use a language-independent "pseudocode"; this has few (if any) grammar rules, but there is enough structure to describe the processes carried out by a program. Thus we can avoid the confusion of syntax structures but still be able to describe the action of a program.

I'll define the basic building blocks of such a pseudocode in this chapter; we shall use it throughout the rest of the book to construct easy to understand descriptions of computer programs.

Assignment

We use the symbol ← to mean "takes the value of". Our simple sum in pseudocode becomes:

total ← bill + tax

ie, total takes the value of the sum of bill and tax.

Note that this form of assignment is destructive – in other words, it destroys the original value held by the label total, and replaces it with the computed sum (bill + tax).

Command sequences

A computer program consists of a series of statements (instructions), arranged in a defined order; when the computer carries it out (executes it), actions are performed. The order of the statements, and therefore the order of the actions that follow, defines the processing function of the program.

Statements may be simple or compound. Simple statements contain a single action or command, eg READ next-number; compound statements comprise several commands in one.

The sequence operator

We call a group of statements in a compound that the system must carry out in a particular order a command sequence. For instance:

READnextnumberPRINTthatnumberREADnextnumberPRINTthatnumber

Without proper punctuation, we find it hard to make sense of this. Also, in order to execute the correct sequence, the computer must know when one statement ends and the next begins. This is not always obvious. Therefore we need a sequencing operator to mark each statement. Each program language has its own sequence operator; so in pseudocode we shall use the semi-colon (;) between statements. That makes the above sequence:

READ next-number; PRINT that-number; READ next-number; PRINT that-number;

However, it is not good programming practice to put more than one statement on a line – this can lead to all sorts of problems in the future. The sequencing becomes even clearer if we enter each statement on a new line:

READ next-number;

PRINT that-number;

READ next-number;

PRINT that-number;

Input, output and arithmetic

A computer program must obviously be able to get data from and send data to the outside world (eg, the user); so we need a few key words to allow this:

READ   to input data from a disk or tape eg READ next-number;

WRITE   to output data to a disk or tape eg WRITE stock-record;

ACCEPT   to input data from a keyboard eg ACCEPT operator-response;

DISPLAY   to output data to a screen eg DISPLAY error-message;

PRINT   to output data to a printer eg PRINT name, address, phone;

Pseudocode allows basic arithmetic, using the standard arithmetic operators and comparators:

+ addition	= equal to	
− subtraction	> greater than	>= greater than or equal to
* multiplication	< less than	<= less than or equal to
/ division	<> not equal to	

Making comments

Most statements within a computer program are executable. This means they define something the program must actually do. Other statements are not executable; for instance, they define data structures, or describe aspects of the program to the human reader. This last class of statements is known as the comment.

Long comments describe large data structures or command sequences; we write these in block format:

/*

* This is a long comment in block format.

*

* In this example note that the opening slash-star and closing

* star-slash are on lines by themselves.

*

* Note also that an asterisk appears before each

* line of comment text, and that all the comments

* line up in column two.

*

* Blank comment lines aid legibility.

*

*/

Short comments may go on a single line, eg to describe individual data declarations or statements:

INTEGER status; /* 0 = FAIL ; 1 = PASS ; */

Use comments freely to describe what is happening within a program; but remember to update them whenever you change the associated statements.

1.3 MORE ADVANCED PROGRAM STRUCTURES

Looping the loop

An important sequence control technique is the loop (iteration); this allows the program to work through the same command sequence a number of times. Loop statements may take two special forms:

Repeat {... command sequence ...} until some condition is true

or

While some condition is true do {... command sequence ...}

The REPEAT loop

We write the REPEAT ... UNTIL construct as follows :

REPEAT

command sequence;

UNTIL condition;

This will cycle through the command sequence until the specified condition becomes true. The actual "condition" is a logical expression whose value can be either True or False. Examples are end of file?, new page?, and so on.

Note how I indent (space in) the command sequence between REPEAT and UNTIL. This is to stress their significance within the loop. Here is a full example.

REPEAT

    READ next-number;

    PRINT next-number;

UNTIL end-of-number-list;

This will repeatedly copy numbers from a list on tape or disk to the printer – until there are no more numbers left.

The main feature of the REPEAT ... UNTIL construct is that it tests the condition at the end of the loop. Therefore it carries out the command sequence at least once. Thus, in the above case, the program reads and prints the next number before it checks for "end-of-number-list". This raises an obvious problem: what happens if the input number list is empty? In such a case, READ next-number could not do anything sensible, and the result could be that the program fails.

More suitable would be to check for end-of-number-list first. The WHILE loop can do this.

The WHILE loop

The WHILE ... DO construct tests the condition at the start of the loop. If the condition is true, the program carries out the command sequence and then repeats the test. Otherwise it ignores the command sequence. We write it as follows:

WHILE condition

    DO

      command sequence;

    ENDO;

The previous example becomes:

WHILE NOT end-of-number-list

    DO

      READ next-number;

      PRINT next-number;

    ENDO;

Now there is no problem with an empty number list.

The FOR loop

The FOR loop is a special case of the WHILE ... DO construct; here the condition clause defines how many times the program should pass through the loop.

FOR i FROM a to b	FOR index FROM 1 to 5
DO	DO
command sequence;	PRINT index;
ENDO;	ENDO;

Here i is the loop control variable used to control carrying out the command sequence the required number of times. An optional extension to the conditional clause within the FOR loop is to step it from the starting value to the final value:

FOR i FROM a to b STEP x

allows the value of i to change by some value other than 1 each time round.

Branching

Another important sequence control technique is the conditional branch (or selection) construct. This involves the IF statement and its variations, and also the CASE statement.

Simple branches

The simplest form of the IF statement allows the program either to carry out or ignore the command sequence – depending on whether or not the specified condition is true:

IF condition	IF new-page
THEN	THEN
command sequence;	PRINT headings;
ENDIF;	ENDIF;

Note the ENDIF term which marks where the IF statement stops.

An obvious extension to this simple one-way selection is the two-way "either/or" branch:

IF condition	IF page-number is odd
THEN	THEN
command sequence 1;	PRINT page-number on left;
ELSE	ELSE
command sequence 2;	PRINT page-number on right;
ENDIF;	ENDIF;

This will execute command sequence 1 if the condition is true, otherwise Command Sequence 2.

Multiple branching

We can further extend this IF-THEN-ELSE construct to allow multiple selections, by replacing one (or more) of the command sequences by nested IF statements:

```
IF condition 1                          IF choice is "E"
    THEN                                    THEN
       command sequence 1;                     RUN enquiry-program;
    ELSE IF condition 2                     ELSE IF choice is "U"
        THEN                                    THEN
           command sequence 2;                     RUN update-prgram;
        ELSE IF condition 3                     ELSE IF choice is . . .
            THEN . . .                              THEN . . .
              :                                        :
            ELSE IF condition N                     ELSE IF choice is "X"
                THEN                                    THEN
                   command sequence N;                     EXIT menu-selection;
                ELSE                                    ELSE
                   default command sequence;               DISPLAY error-message;
ENDIF;                                  ENDIF;
```

Here, if any of the conditions 1 ... N is true, the program carries out the corresponding command sequence. Otherwise it follows the default command sequence (if any). If more than one condition is true, only the first one the program meets in the nested sequence will be executed. Programmers must take care to ensure that each ELSE clause correctly matches the corresponding IF THEN. Indentation helps to achieve this, and makes the code not only more readable but also easier to check. We can also use nested IF statements within THEN clauses as well as in ELSE clauses.

Note

Each IF statement should have a corresponding ENDIF, but at the end of a series of multiple branches this often results in a series of ENDIFs, which can take up many lines. Where this is the case then for brevity, we have used only one ENDIF, which corresponds to the first IF in the multiple branch. You can do this if you think that the resulting code is understandable, or you can include all the ENDIFs if you think that this makes the logic clearer.

Just in CASE

We use the CASE ... ENDCASE construct (sometimes known as a Switch) when we need to select from several independent branches (as with the menu choice sequence we looked at above). Each case is mutually exclusive, and each condition is independent. Selection involves comparing the value of the case index (value) with the values given in turn: if the program finds a match, it carries out the corresponding command sequence; if it finds no match, it works on the (optional) default command sequence. This construct is much easier to read than several nested IFs, as you can now see.

DO CASE OF index	DO CASE OF menu-choice
CASE index condition 1	CASE "E"
command sequence 1;	RUN enquiry-program;
CASE index condition 2	CASE "U"
command sequence 2;	RUN update-program;
CASE index condition ...	CASE ...
:	:
CASE index condition N	CASE "X"
command sequence N;	EXIT menu;
OTHERWISE	OTHERWISE
default command sequence;	DISPLAY error message;
ENDCASE;	ENDCASE;

Note that not all program languages support the CASE structure.

Conditionals

All the above sequence control constructs use a conditional clause to control how a program carries out command sequences in loops or branches. Each condition is a logical expression whose value can be either True or False. Thus it forms the basis of the program's "decision" of whether or not to execute a given command sequence.

Conditional clauses may be simple or compound:

simple

IF new-page THEN ...

compound

IF mark > 60 AND exam = "science" THEN ...

Simple conditions

A simple condition consists of two constants, variables, or arithmetic expressions linked by the symbols:

=   >   >=   <   <=   <>

See the list above for their meanings if you can't remember. Below are some examples of simple conditions.

> mark >= 60
>
> interest − 90 > limit
>
> answer = "yes"

Compound conditions

This statement:

> IF mark > 60 AND subject = "science" OR mark > 70 THEN ...

means:

> "If the mark is greater than 60 and the subject is science, or if the mark is greater than 70, then ..."

Brackets make complex expressions more readable and help avoid confusion:

> IF (mark > 60 AND subject = "science") OR (mark > 70) THEN ...

New procedures

Blocks

So far we have looked at the single statements which together make up a program. The system then carries out as a single logical sequence. However, with all but the smallest programs, it is wise to split it up in order to reduce its complexity. We break down programs into blocks or modules; each contains a limited number of instructions.

You have probably noticed that in our pseudocode examples we have ended each command with an END statement. That is important in this idea of modules or blocks.

The basic block structure is a single statement such as:

> WHILE ...
>   DO
>   ....
>   ....
>   ENDO;

or an assignment:

count ← 0;

or, more likely, a compound statement such as

IF condition-fail

   THEN

     PERFORM block-1;

   ELSE

     PERFORM block-2;

ENDIF;

We can combine sets of basic blocks into bigger and bigger blocks, and then, if it helps, we can assign a name to the block. This lets us refer to the entire block as a single object, as in:

PERFORM block-1;

As far as our pseudocode is concerned, we will use this method to refer to blocks of statements that we have defined somewhere away from the code currently being written. As an example, Program-1 in Figure 1.1 consists of three calls to external blocks (sub-routines), called Start, Main, and End; all of them have been defined somewhere else.

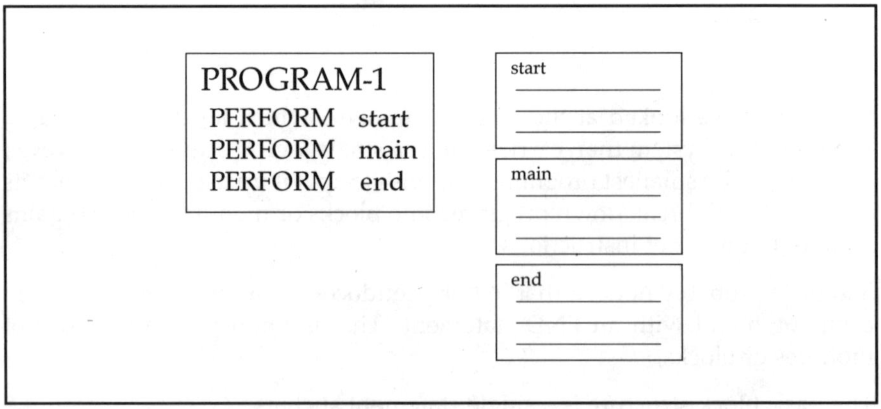

Figure 1.1   External sub-routines

In almost every computer language, blocks appear either between special words (BEGIN ... END, for instance), or in special structures such as "paragraphs", "sections", "procedures", or "sub-routines". Thus when you translate pseudocode blocks into an actual computer language, the choice of structure will depend on the language concerned.

In COBOL, for instance, there are two ways to define a block. The first method involves defining code kept within the rest of the program; the second method uses procedures (sometimes called sub-routines) that go into store separately from the main program, and are activated by calls as required.

For example, in Figure 1.2, Program-one contains blocks defined inside the control code: this is called "in-line" code. Program-two, on the other hand, uses procedures.

PROGRAM-ONE

   begin
   ———————————
   ———————————
   ———————————

     begin
     —————————
     —————————

     end
    —————
    —————

     begin
     ———
    end
 end

PROGRAM-TWO

  PARA-ONE
    PERFORM PARA-READ;
    PERFORM PARA-WRITE;

  PARA-READ
   ———————
   ———————

  PARA-WRITE
   ———————
   ———————
   ———————

Figure 1.2   In-line and external sub-routines

Either way, we can transfer our pseudocode descriptions with little effort into almost any computer language, as in Figure 1.3.

One feature of the block system is that it often lets you define and declare data values for use only within a given block. Variables defined this way are "local" variables; in contrast ones used throughout the program are "global" variables. For example, Figure 1.4 shows you can use the same label inside a block and outside it. This is because when we define a block any local label always supersedes a global one with the same name. Thus global labels operate in any block inside the one in which they are defined – unless there is a local label with the same name. On the other hand, you can use no local variables outside the block in which they are defined.

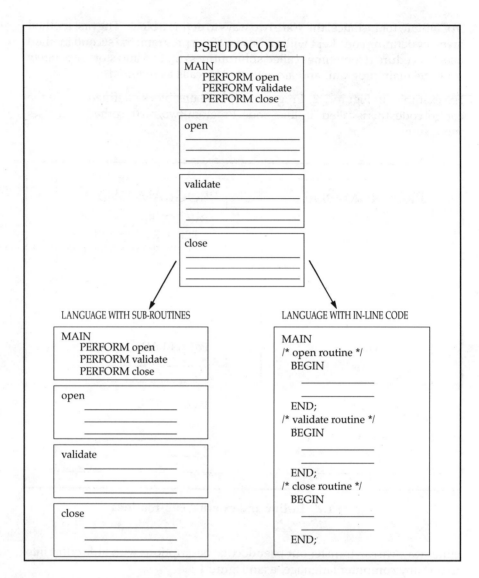

Figure 1.3 Translation of pseudocode

```
BEGIN
        NUMBER : INTEGER;  ◄──────────── global variable
            BEGIN
            NAME : CHARACTER;
            NUMBER : REAL;  ◄──────── local variable
        END;
    END;
```

Figure 1.4 Global and local variables

We call languages that allow you to define blocks in-line "block-structured": the most famous of these is ALGOL. Having the code kept in-line makes it easier to follow the program logic. Not all languages are like this, for example the 1968 and 1974 versions of COBOL. In these cases, we have to use separately located sub-routines to control and protect the variables used inside them; this can make it hard for people to follow the code in a long program. COBOL85 introduced the option of putting the code from sub-routines either inside the program or separate from it.

Parameter passing

So far we have seen that a simple program consists of a series of instructions in a linear sequence, ie one after another; more complex programs often split into smaller units called blocks (which we will sometimes refer to later as "modules"), each having a separate task.

Dividing a program up this way has several advantages. First, the overall program which would otherwise be too complex for people to understand (and therefore later amend), is simplified to such an extent that we can handle each part in isolation quite easily.

Second, while we could write out the same routine in the program several times as necessary, say for printing out data, it would be inefficient, wasteful and boring to do so. So those routines used in more than one place appear only once, stored somewhere outside the main code of the program and called up whenever needed. Sometimes, people collect often-used routines into "libraries". These may consist of routines used on a single site for consistency in, for instance, screen design, or be international, like the NAG Fortran Library (which contains mathematical and scientific functions not included as standard in FORTRAN).

Some externally held routines can work without having any data passed to them, and without sending any back – generally, however, they need some data to work with, even for a simple operation. For example, a routine to print the value of a variable needs the label of the variable to ensure it uses the correct data. We call the information passed a "parameter". Sometimes the parameter is simply a label, as in COBOL:

CALL   print-rec

　　USING

　　　　record-1.

Sometimes the system needs the label and its associated data type is needed, as in Ada:

INCREMENT(INTEGER(R));

With a language like COBOL85 the position of each label in the parameter list is important, as you can rename the variables in the sub-routine (and thus make them local). This lets a sub-routine work on any data, regardless of the labels used; the programmer can pass just a copy of the variable to the sub-routine so that the original data is protected. See Figure 1.5.

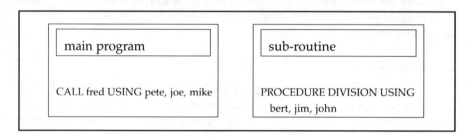

Figure 1.5   Parameter passing

Recursive procedures

Recursion involves looping an indefinite number of times through a sequence or procedure. It differs from the loops described earlier in that the programmer does not know the number of cycles required at the time of writing (as with REPEAT and WHILE) – and the command sequence calls itself until the condition controlling it becomes true. Recursion can provide a very elegant and efficient (if sometimes hard to follow) solution to certain kinds of problem.

Recursion involves two stages:

(a)   If the problem has been simplified as far as it can, this is the solution.

(b)   Otherwise (a) is a way to move one step nearer to the simplest case.

This may not seem to be much of a solution to a problem, but an example should make it clearer. Imagine you need to get-the-bottom-book-from-the-pile; the solution would be:

<u>get-the-bottom-book-from-the-pile</u>

(a)   If there is only one book on the pile, take it – this is the one you want = simplest case.

(b)   Otherwise take off the top book, put it aside then get-the-bottom-book-from-the-pile remaining = a step nearer to (a).

The advantage is that you do not need to know the size of the pile of books – the routine will call itself until the condition at (a) is true.

There is a danger with recursion – use with care because you may create an infinite loop if you define the condition controlling the execution badly. Partly because of this, some languages (such as COBOL) do not allow recursion.

1.4 PSEUDOCODE SUMMARY

(a)   The assignment symbol "← " means "takes the value of":

C ← A + B

means C takes the value of A plus B.

(b)   The sequencing operator delimits each statement in a compound:

DO this; DO that; DO the-other;

(c)   Key words allow data input to and output from the program:

READ to input data from a backing store, eg READ next-number;

WRITE to output data to backing store, eg WRITE stock-record;

ACCEPT to input data from a keyboard, eg ACCEPT operator-response;

DISPLAY to output data to a screen, eg DISPLAY error-report;

PRINT to output data to a printer, eg PRINT name, code

(d)   There are various looping constructs:

REPEAT

command sequence;

UNTIL condition;

WHILE condition

DO

command sequence;

ENDO;

FOR i FROM a to b (STEP x)

DO

command sequence;

ENDO;

(e)   Conditional branching may use the IF-THEN-ELSE construct:

IF condition

THEN

```
                command sequence 1;
            ELSE
                command sequence 2;
        ENDIF;
We obtain multiple branching (or selection) with nested IFs:
        IF condition 1
            THEN
                command sequence 1;
            ELSE IF condition 2
                    THEN
                        command sequence 2;
                    ELSE IF condition 3
                            THEN ...

                    :

                            ELSE
                                default command sequence;
        ENDIF;
Or we can use the (better) CASE structure:
        DO CASE OF index
            CASE index condition 1
                command sequence 1;
            CASE index condition 2
                command sequence 2;
            CASE index condition ...

                :

            CASE index condition N
                command sequence N;
            OTHERWISE
                default command sequence;
                ENDCASE;
```

(F) We call procedures using the PERFORM or CALL key words:

```
        PERFORM label; or
        CALL label;
```

NOW TRY THESE . . .

Exercise One

Write assignment statements for:

a) assigning the value 257 to the memory variable "HOUSE NUMBER"

b) initialising the variable "COUNTRY" with the name of your country

c) entering the date into a set of three variables comprising: "DAY", "MONTH" and "YEAR"

d) decreasing the variable "NUMBER" by 3

e) dividing PERCENTAGE by 2.

Exercise Two

Write the statement which will allow:

a) the DAY-OF-WEEK and WEEK-NUMBER to be input

b) the NAME and BIRTHPLACE to be output to a monitor

c) the SUBJECT and EXAM-MARK to be printed on the printer.

Exercise Three

a) write statements to take in two numbers, then print the smaller as a percentage of the larger

b) write a program that will change fahrenheit temperatures into centigrade.

Exercise Four

An exam marking system works as follows:

exam mark	grade
less than 40	4
a minimum of 40 but less than 50	3
at least 50 but less than 70	2
at least 70	1

Design a program that will input the EXAM-MARK and display the EXAM-MARK and GRADE on the screen.

2   Data and data structures

OBJECTIVES

When you have worked through this chapter, you should be able to:

- distinguish between numeric, string and logical data
- distinguish between constant and variable data
- use data structure diagrams to show data items and their sub-division, including alternative sub-items
- use such diagrams to show the structures of a file and of an array
- explain the concept of indexing in the case of arrays
- compare the logical and physical structures of a typical record of static data, and compare these in turn with those of a linked list, ring and net
- explain the concept of pointers with reference to linked data structures
- outline algorithms for searching tables for specific data items in different contexts
- outline the algorithm of the logarithmic search (binary search)
- outline a simple alogorithm for sorting the elements of a list (one-dimensional array).

INTRODUCTION

Computing is a crucial field within information technology (IT). IT concerns the effective handling of information for the good of society. Effective handling, in turn, means the storage, processing, transfer and presentation of information.

Any IT system handles information in some physical form, eg electric pulses or dots of magnetism. In such a form, the information has no meaning, and we now call it data. So IT and (in particular) computing involve the handling of data – and it is the task of the software to make that handling as efficient and effective as possible.

Efficient and effective data handling leads to the need to see data as in any of a number of different "structures". Say you want your program to accept from the user information about a number of customer orders (eg, name, address, items ordered with prices, etc); it should then process these data items to produce an invoice. To develop such a program, you need to describe not only the program structures (which we looked at in the last chapter), but the data structures too.

Now, therefore, we look at the basic concepts of data and data structures.

2.1 TYPES OF DATA

There are two fundamental types (or kinds) of data: numeric and non-numeric. Numeric data consists essentially of numbers – used for such things as sums of money, ages, distances. Non-numeric data involves "non"-numbers – such as strings of characters that stand for names and addresses. We can see the difference between these two basic data types in the case of the number 13. When a program carries out an arithmetic operation on the number, it stores it as numeric data (binary 1101, in fact); however, when it prints "13" on paper, it stores the information as non-numeric data (character "1" followed by character "3").

Numeric data

We divide numeric data items into two main groups: INTEGERS and REALS. Integers are whole numbers, used to count things (eg the number of days in the year, or of oranges in a basket). Real numbers may have a fraction part – we use them to measure things like the length of a piece of string, or the cost of an item in dollars. Most commercial numeric data can be adequately described using these two main types; however, some uses in science need a further type of numeric data – the COMPLEX number; this is beyond the scope of this book.

In other words, integers are whole numbers such as 1, 2, 3, ...; they can be positive or negative, and count discrete objects such as numbers of bananas. Integers are precise: the integer value 13 means exactly 13.

Reals are fractional numbers (1.0, 234.66, ...); they too can be positive or negative, and measure things like the length of a piece of string. Reals may not be precise (exact): an IT system may store the real number 13 as 13.000000 or perhaps as 12.999999.

Non-numeric data

Most non-numeric data are character strings (like "Hallo!"), or logical values (to stand for True/False conditions). Other non-numeric data types exist, such as pointers (which store addresses of variables) and dates (which allow arithmetic operations on calendar dates).

Character strings, as their name suggests, are sequences of data items of type CHARACTER (or CHAR); we usually have to put them in double quotes (") as in "Success". Strings may include any printable character, and are stored as codes (using the ASCII or EBCDIC code system, for instance). Program languages, such as COBOL, designed for working with characters, may further classify character data as numeric (the digits 0 – 9, the signs + and −, the decimal point), alphabetic (letters A – Z, a – z, spaces), or alphanumeric (all printable characters). Do not confuse the numeric character type with the numeric data type – the ASCII character "1" (binary 0011 0001) is not the same as the integer value 1 (binary 0000 0001).

Since systems store characters as exact (coded) integer values, they can compare them directly. Thus:

A < Z   "ABC" > "AAA"   "Alpha" < "Alphabet"

These examples show the basic rules for comparison of character strings in the case of most program languages:

-   the order is space (" ") < A < B < ... < Y < Z, with lower case > UPPER CASE

-   string comparisons take place character by character, leftmost first

-   the string with the first larger character value is the greater.

We can also concatenate strings (ie, join them to create longer strings), and select character sequences, eg "March" from "19 March 1991".

Constants and variables

We met variables in Chapter 1. In IT they are really storage cells (places or locations) whose contents may change when a program runs. We refer to these storage cells (and their contents) by their labels (names); we generally choose these to reflect the contents or usage of that variable: eg gross-salary, tax-rate. (Note that label rules vary with language.)

Variables may be numeric or non-numeric – the storage cells may contain any of the data types discussed above. However, once you have declared or defined a label for data of a specific data type, then normally only data of that declared type may go in that cell. Constants are "read-only" variables – storage cells containing fixed data values which cannot change during a program run.

We can use constants and variables in numeric and non-numeric expressions. In other words, we can put a constant into a variable, as long as they are both the same type.

2.2 DATA STRUCTURES

All data has structure. That means we can link individual data items into larger data units with some further meaning. Here is an example.

An address book is a data structure containing data items (name, address, phone number) logically grouped together to give information about an individual.

Each data item may itself be a group of simpler data items. Thus the address consists of data items for house, street, town. Again each of these data items may contain even simpler ones — for instance the street name may consist of several words. The simplest data items in a structure (in this case, characters) are known as primitives; we use these to build up fields (spaces for data) containing meaningful information. Thus the character "L" does not mean much, but the string "Lagos" identifies a city.

Structure diagrams

We can show the grouping and relationship of data items in a real case in picture form using data structure diagrams. Each data item shows as a box containing the label, as in Figure 2.1. Figure 2.2 shows how to sub-divide a data item into its parts.

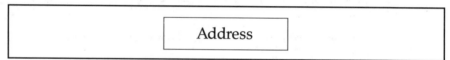

Figure 2.1   A data item

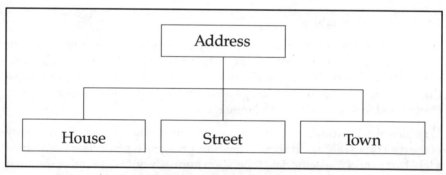

Figure 2.2   Sub-division

This tells us that address consists of three items, one each of house, street, town, and in that order (left to right). We call such an arrangement a sequence.

Sometimes we need to show that the contents of a particular structure element (item) may be one of a number of possibilities. For this, we use a small circle in the top right hand corner of each box; for instance, house may be either a number or a name, but not both. See Figure 2.3.

Putting these left to right has no special meaning. However, if we mark one sub-element as an alternative, all the sub-elements of that item must appear the same way. Often we need to create "dummy" sub-elements to maintain this structure;

thus a phone number may consist of an area code and a subscriber number, with either a national or international code in front. See Figure 2.4.

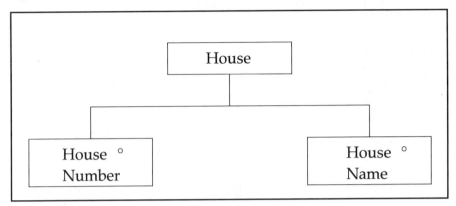

Figure 2.3   Selection

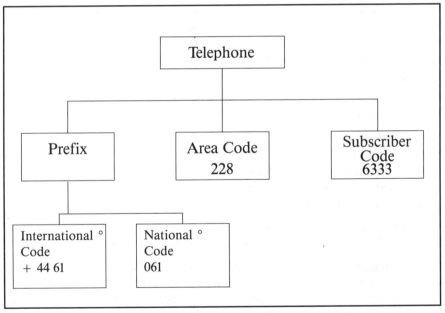

Figure 2.4   Ordering of alternatives

Data items are often repeated. The symbol for this is a star (*) in the top right hand corner; it means the data item is repeated zero or more times. Thus, in the example of Figure 2.5, there may be several middle names – or none at all. We call this an iteration.

We can show any combination of data, no matter how complex, as an upside-down tree (to use the common name); each lower level describes the levels above in more detail. If we now put our examples together, we can see how to describe each address book. Look at Figure 2.6 for this.

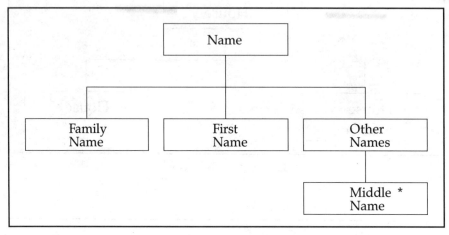

Figure 2.5   Iteration

In computer terms the whole address book is a file; the entry for each person is a record.

The value of the data structure picture is enormous; there are many areas of program design in which people use it.

First, once we have drawn as a tree the structure and interrelationships of the data to be processed, it is much more easy to check against the specification than is a narrative description (one in words). If, during this checking, you find that an item or element has been missed out, it is easy to add to the structure diagram without re-drawing.

Secondly, if you realise that you have not included enough detail for any item, you can add it by extending the diagram down from the correct point.

Thirdly, in general, the structure of a program will closely follow the structure of the data it is to process. Each element of the data structure diagram stands for a data item which will need some kind of processing. Thus, for each element of the data structure diagram there will be an appropriate program component. Further, if there is a repetition in the data structure, there will be a need for a suitable loop in the program; a selection implies a selection element; and so on.

2.3   ARRAYS AND TABLES

We have now seen that, however complex a data structure might be, we can always show it on paper by a structure diagram that we can then easily convert

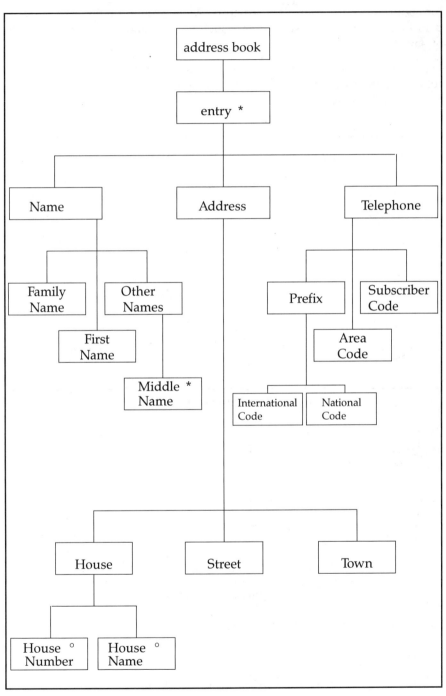

Figure 2.6 Complete address book

(or code) into a program data structure. Most program languages provide definitions of simple data structures – such as arrays and tables, which are lists of data items.

Let us discuss a stock item in a garage, a car part available in four different colours. To record the stock level for each colour requires four separate variables, as Figure 2.7 shows.

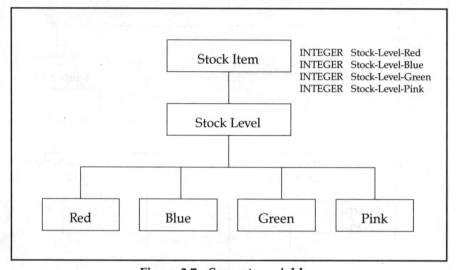

Figure 2.7   Separate variables

We can group these variables in an array of four elements. The value of each integer element records the Stock Level, and the order shows the colour; look at Figure 2.8 for this.

Stock Level Array	Integer 1 Value 6	Integer 2 Value 4	Integer 3 Value 7	Integer 4 Value 8
	(red)	(blue)	(green)	(pink)

Figure 2.8   Array

We would code this as follows:

COBOL	STOCK-LEVEL PIC 9(4) OCCURS 4 TIMES.
Ada	stock-level : array (1..4) of INTEGER;
C	INTEGER stock-level [4];

We refer to the contents of the storage cell of each array element by a "subscript" or "index". For instance, stock-level(3) has the value 7, showing that there are seven (green) items on the shelf.

This array has one dimension – it is a simple list. We can extend it from one dimension to two or more dimensions; then it can hold more information. For an example, see Figure 2.9.

	red (1)	blue (2)	green (3)	pink (4)
Stock Level (1) (FRANCE)	Integer Value 6	Integer Value 4	Integer Value 7	Integer Value 4
Stock Level (2) (UK)	Integer Value 5	Integer Value 2	Integer Value 4	Integer Value 5

Figure 2.9   Two-dimensional array

The COBOL code is:

```
03 STOCK-ITEM OCCURS 4 TIMES
   05 STOCK-LEVEL OCCURS 2 TIMES
      07 STOCK-VALUE PIC 9(4).
```

2.4   FILES AND RECORDS

The data structures (arrays, tables) so far discussed reflect simple groupings of data in a computer program: designed to make processing the data easier. As data structures become more complex, their relationships also become more complex; as a result, they require further organisation into larger groups of related data items – such as linked lists, records, and files. Now we shall look at records and files in more detail than before.

A data record is a group of related items we can treat as a single group. Thus the name, address, phone number of someone in the address book we looked at earlier are related facts which form a group, or record, in the address book or the corresponding computer file. We have already seen that these related items (or data fields) may themselves consist of smaller data items (as the address field may contain house, street and town items).

Data records may group to form files. These are well defined data structures that contain related data organised in convenient groupings (records) of data items; it is easy to store a file on, for instance, magnetic tape or disk for future use. We can show this higher level organisation of data as in Figure 2.10.

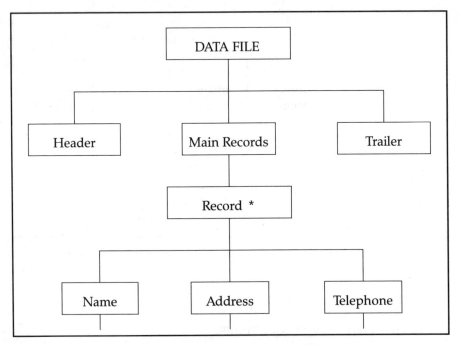

Figure 2.10   Files and records

Note that this data structure diagram has two additional types of data record: headers and trailers. Header records keep apart different groups of records (as we may divide the address book into sections for friends, relatives, colleagues), each with its own header. Trailer records contain codes to mark the end of a set of data.

Some address books have an index for easy access to individual entries; a data file may use a "key" for the same purpose. Each record then has a special key field for easy access to that record. For instance, the name field in the address book file is an obvious choice.

As with arrays, the structure diagram again shows how to code this data. Thus, in COBOL, conversion to a record is simple, as the depth of a data item from the root (top) of the tree gives its level number. The only information about the data not included in the diagram is the size and range of each element – but this will be available from the file specification documentation which should be supplied to the programmer by the systems analyst.

Going back to the address book example, the complete data structure looks like Figure 2.11.

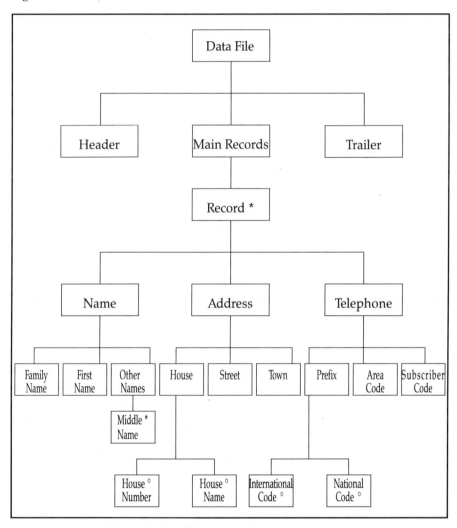

Figure 2.11 Address book – data structure

We can see that if the record is level 1, then name, address and phone will be level 2; family-name, first-name, other-names, house, street, town, prefix, area-code, subscriber-code will be level 3; and, finally, middle name, house-number, house-name, international-code and national-code will be level 4. Using this as the basis, and ignoring the size of each item for now, a suitable COBOL description would be as in the box.

01 NAME-ADDR-RECORD

02 NAME	02 ADDRESS	02 TELEPHONE
03 FAMILY PIC ***	03 HOUSE	03 PREFIX
03 FIRST PIC ***	04 NUMBER PIC ***	04 INTERNATIONAL PIC ***
03 OTHER PIC ***	04 NAME PIC ***	04 NATIONAL PIC ***
04 MIDDLE PIC ***		03 AREA PIC ***
		03 SUBSCRIBER PIC ***

2.5   LINKED LISTS

Records and files relate to data which is fixed at the time that the program processes it. This is "static" data – it stays the same size throughout the program run (eg, a table containing fifty prices).

Sometimes, however, it is not possible to decide in advance what the size of the data structure will be. Take, for instance, a program which regulates the temperature of an oven to allow foods to cook at different speeds. The program will sample the temperature less often when the oven is cool, than when it approaches the critical value. Thus the size of the data structure needed to store information about the temperature will change as the program runs. Because it changes, we call it a "dynamic" data structure.

Files and records, even arrays and tables, do not suit this kind of application, as the programmer will not know the size of the area needed to store the data before the program runs. The solution is to use something called a linked list; this will allow new records to be created as and when needed.

The one problem with dynamic data structures is how to find out where the next data item is inside the computer's store. This problem does not apply to static structures – the physical position of data items also corresponds to their logical sequence; look, for example, at the record in Figure 2.12. Its physical structure in the computer's store is as shown in Figure 2.13.

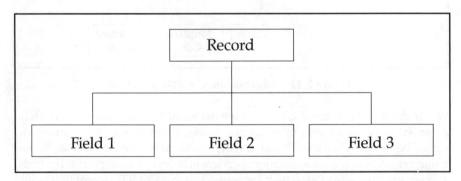

Figure 2.12   Static data – logical structure

Figure 2.13 Static data – physical structure

Thus when the program allocates data storage space in the computer's main store, it uses the data declarations to reserve an area for each record and field. When a linked list is required this will not be possible (the ultimate size is unknown); as an alternative, data is written to the store in any cell that is available. However, so that the program can also retrieve it, the address of the next record is written into the last record processed – which is where the "link" of the name comes in. Thus each record links to the one before and the one after. See Figure 2.14.

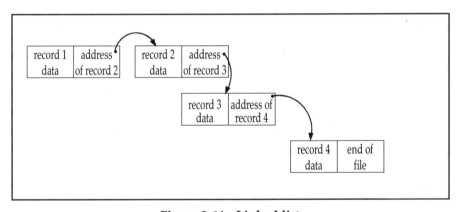

Figure 2.14 Linked list

Not all program languages offer the linked list. One that does is Ada – it needs the facility as it is a real-time language (that is, one used to write programs to monitor and control events in the real world, like the action of an oven or a lift). COBOL, on the other hand, doesn't have the facility as it works mainly in batch mode, with data input as individual records, whose size and format are fixed in advance.

Sometimes we can form a linked list into a closed loop which begins and ends in the same place. This data structure is a ring; where several rings overlap they are together known as a net. Nets are important in data base systems. For instance, we could structure a library of books by class (subject), author and title, as in Figure 2.15.

Each part of the structure forms a ring. If you were to search the system for a book by Deeson on fax machines, the search would start at the class level for computers, then the authors would be checked for Deeson, and finally the individual books for that author would be checked for the exact subject required. Note that if the search fails at any stage, the ring/net structure ensures that the query ends up back at the start.

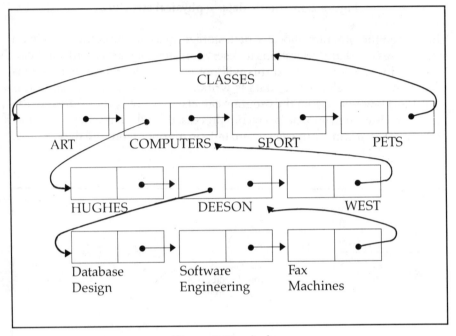

Figure 2.15   A ring

2.6   MANIPULATING DATA

Pointers and indexes

We have now seen that we can arrange data in a variety of ways inside the computer's store. Static structures exist such as files, records, tables and arrays, as well as dynamic ones like linked lists.

The one thing all these structures have in common is that they all use pointers. Thus the "links" of linked lists are the addresses of records: the address part of the record "points" to the address of the next record, so is one kind of pointer. With arrays and tables the subscript (or index) acts as another kind of pointer, showing the position in the whole array or table of each data item. Finally, certain kinds of files have indexes to identify where in the file each record is stored; again this is a kind of pointer.

Indexes are a special sort of pointer as they relate only to fixed data structures like files, arrays and tables; ordinary pointers are much more flexible, as we will now see.

Searching for data

Often, during processing, it becomes necessary to search a table for an item which matches some known key information. It may be that the table contains, for example, product description codes, together with other information about each product.

There are many ways of conducting a search, or a "table look-up"; they depend on such factors as the number and size of entries in the table, and whether or not the data stored is fixed or can vary during the program run (as in the case of a list of variable names generated during compilation of a source program).

The simplest and most obvious approach is to use a linear search; here the program looks at each table element in turn, starting with the first, until either it finds a match or it reaches the end of the table (in which case the key element was "missing", in other words, not in the table). It is usual for all elements of the table to have the same fixed size, so it is relatively simple to describe a standard technique for the linear table search. There are two variants of this technique, depending on whether or not the number of entries in the table is known.

Searching a table of known length

Let us assume that the size of the table (number of entries) is held in a variable called tab-size, the search object is in key, and the table is an array called table, having tab-size elements. Figure 2.16 shows a process to find the position of key in table.

```
for index from 1 to TABSIZE
    do
        if KEY = TABLE [index]
            then goto FOUND;
        endif;
    endo;
MISSING: {process missing key value}
FOUND:   {index contains position in TABLE of value
          which matches KEY}
```

Figure 2.16   Table search (1)

This process will always work, regardless of how the information is ordered in the table; however, for large tables (greater than about a hundred elements), it will take a long time (particularly if many missing keys have to be searched for). If it is known in advance that certain key values occur more often than others, it is a good idea to store these values at the front of the table to speed up finding them.

To make our table search more elegant, and easier to amend, we could rewrite it using two logical items "searching" and "found". The conditional expression "if found" means "if the value of logical item found is true". When you are familiar with logical items, you could actually write "if found is true", if that helps – our language has no restrictions, remember. Similarly "while searching" means "while searching has the value true". Now our process looks like Figure 2.17.

```
index ← 1;
searching ← true ;
while searching
   do
     if KEY = TABLE [index]
       then
           searching ← false;
           found ← true;
       else if index = TABSIZE
           then
               searching ← false;
               found ← false;
           else
               index ← index + 1;
     endif;
   endo;
if found
   then   process record in TABLE [index];
   else   process missing KEY value;
endif;
```

Figure 2.17   Table search (2)

If the information is in the table in order, missing keys may be rejected earlier by determining whether or not the program has come across a key of higher value. This technique, of course, places an extra test within the search loop, and this may remove the advantage of earlier rejection. Figure 2.18 shows the search process without logical items, and Figure 2.19 shows it with them. (Both 2.18 and 2.19 assume that the elements of table are stored in ascending order.)

```
for index from 1 to TABSIZE
  do
      if KEY = TABLE [index]
        then goto FOUND;
            else if KEY < TABLE [index]
                  then {exit from 'do' loop};
                  endif;
      endo;
MISSING: {process missing key value};
FOUND:   {index contains position in TABLE of value which matches
          KEY};
```

Figure 2.18   Table search (3)

```
index ← 1;
searching ← true:
while searching
  do
    if KEY = TABLE [index]
      then
          searching ← false;
          found ← true;
      else if KEY < TABLE [index]
      then
          searching ← false;
          found ← false;
            else if index = TABSIZE
                  then
                    searching ←false;
                    found ← false;
                  else
          index ← index + 1;
      endif;
    endo;
if found
    then process record in TABLE [index];
    else process missing KEY value;
endif;
```

Figure 2.19   Table search (4)

Searching a table of unknown length

If the size of a table is not known, it must contain a special "end-of-table" value. The search then goes on until the program either finds a match or reaches the end-of-table marker (indicating a missing key). This is very similar to the previous example, but instead of looking for an index equal to the table size, we look for a table entry equal to our special end-tab value. Figure 2.20 shows the method.

```
index ← 1;
while KEY <> TABLE [index] and TABLE [index] <> ENDTAB
    do index ← index + 1;
    endo;
if TABLE [index] = KEY
    then {process matching element};
    else {process missing element};
endif;
```

Figure 2.20   Table search (5)

This approach has two obvious advantages. First, we can use it with tables whose number of entries changes during the program run, as long as there is a suitable end-of-table marker after the last legitimate entry.

Second, it minimises the amount of editing required when a program has to be altered to change the size of a fixed-length table, thus minimising the chance of introducing an error. Of course, for such a technique, there must be some kind of "end-of-table" marker. Such a value exists in COBOL as the constant high-values; many other languages have its equivalent. The value is the "highest" value in the sequence of codes used. In ASCII that is the code called DEL. If you have a limited range of permissible values use the highest of these, eg "ZZZ" or 999.

If the table to be searched is larger still, the linear search is perhaps not the most suitable. (Imagine the task of finding a name in the telephone directory using a linear search.) A better approach is to arrange the table entries in order of key value and then use a logarithmic search (sometimes called binary chop).

In this method the program compares the item in the middle of the table with the search key. If they match, then the required entry has been found. If not, the program tests on which side of the target (search key) the examined entry lies. If the table entry is lower in the sequence than the search key, then (because of the ordering of the table) so are all of the preceding entries. On the other hand, if the examined table entry is higher in the sequence, so are all of the following entries.

In either case, we have got rid of half of the table. We can now treat the remaining half table in the same way: half of it (one quarter of the original table) is eliminated. This goes on until either a match is found or, by reducing the area of search to a single entry, the program finds that the required value is not in the table.

Since at each step, we reject one half of the search area, a table of N items will require, at most, $2 \times \log2[sub]N$ comparisons to find a given key or that it is missing. This gives the method its name. The algorithm (pseudocode program) in Figure 2.21 is to search a table of length tab-size for a value which matches key.

```
first ← 1;
last ← TABSIZE;
while first <> last
   do
      interval ← last − first + 1;
      half ← interval / 2;
      pointer ← first + half;
      if KEY = TABLE [pointer]
         then goto FOUND;
      endif;
      {since no match, determine which half of table to keep}
      if KEY > TABLE [pointer]
         then first ← pointer;
         else last ← pointer;
      endif;
   endo;
MISSING: {control comes here if KEY not in TABLE};
FOUND: {process matching element};
```

Figure 2.21 Table search (logarithmic)

Work through this example to see the process better; here we search a table of 1000 items, using a key which matches the 356th entry. Figure 2.22 shows the values in the variables at each step of the search, starting with step 1.

	first	last	continue	pointer	test	result
1:	1	1000	Yes	501	KEY > 501	NO
2:	1	501	Yes	250	KEY > 250	YES
3:	250	501	Yes	376	KEY > 376	NO
4:	250	376	Yes	313	KEY > 313	YES
5:	313	376	Yes	345	KEY > 345	YES
6:	345	376	Yes	361	KEY > 361	YES
7:	361	376	Yes	368	KEY > 368	NO
8:	361	368	Yes	365	match found so stop process	

Figure 2.22   Values found during logarithmic search

From this you can see that the method finds the key in eight attempts – as against the 365 a linear search would need.

Do not forget, though, that we can use the logarithmic search only with an ordered table of values. The overhead of sorting the table entries makes it less suitable for use with tables whose contents vary during program execution, but the method is entirely appropriate for searching large, fixed tables which need to be presorted only once.

2.7   SORTING AND MERGING

Sorting data

This is a complex subject – at this stage we shall look at a simple approach which will suit most applications.

Firstly, note how "internal" and "external" sorting differ. An internal sort involves re-arranging the items of a table so that the values of a particular key are in order (either ascending or descending). Of course, an internal sort can be used only when the main store can hold the entire data set. Where we have to work with large volumes of data, such as massive files, we need an "external" sort. In this book, we regard such an external sort as somebody else's problem, and assume the existence of suitable software to do it.

A simple internal sort

Consider a linear array A having N elements, each holding an integer value. For example if N is 10, the array looks like Figure 2.23.

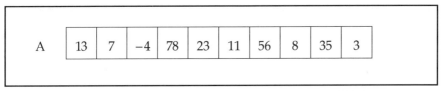

Figure 2.23   Internal sort (1)

Our task is to re-arrange the contents of the array so that the elements are in strict ascending order of value – Figure 2.24.

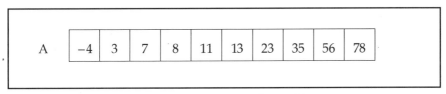

Figure 2.24   Internal sort (2)

This is the way we will do it. We will inspect the full list, looking for the lowest value. Having found it, we exchange that value with the value at the beginning of the list. Now we can ignore the first item in the list, and repeat the operation with the shorter list starting at the second item. Having found the lowest item in that list, we exchange it with the value in position two (the head of the shorter list). We repeat this until we have only two items left, exchange them if necessary – and the sort is complete.

To find the lowest value in a list, we will use two extra variables, svalue and spointer (for smallest-value and smallest-value-pointer). We put the first value in the list into svalue, and its position into spointer. Now we compare svalue with each of the other values in turn; if the value from the list is smaller than svalue, we replace the content of svalue with that smaller value, and note, in spointer, the position from which it came. When we have compared all the items in the list with svalue in this way, we will have the position of the lowest value in spointer. Now exchange the value of the head of the list with the value at spointer. That is one iteration complete.

The process shown in Figure 2.25 will achieve this objective.

By following through a few stages of this process, we can gain a clearer understanding of what is happening.

The original array is in Figure 2.26.

```
for first in range 1 to N-1
   do
      svalue ← A [first];
      spointer ← first;
{svalue will eventually contain value of smallest element,
spointer will contain its position within A – now compare
svalue with all other elements beyond it in A }
for the next in range first + 1 to N
   do
      if A [next] < svalue
         then {remember this smaller value and its position}
            svalue ← A [next];
            spointer ← next;
      endif;
   endo;
{at this stage, svalue will contain the value of the smallest
element, spointer its position}
if spointer <> first
   then {since first element not the smallest exchange smallest
         with first}
      temp ← A [first];
      A [first] ← A [spointer];
      A [spointer]: ← temp;
   endif
endo
{array A now stored into ascending order}
```

Figure 2.25   Sorting the elements of a table

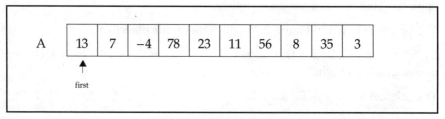

Figure 2.26 Internal sort (3)

The inner loop terminates with svalue = 4 and spointer = 3 (check this!), giving Figure 2.27.

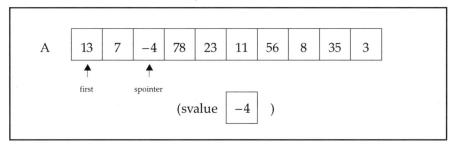

Figure 2.27 Internal sort (4)

The exchange now takes place between the two indicated values (note that we need a third label, temp, for this), leaving the situation as in Figure 2.28.

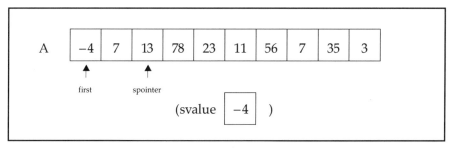

Figure 2.28 Internal sort (5)

Now repeat the outer loop with the value of first moved on by one, Figure 2.29.

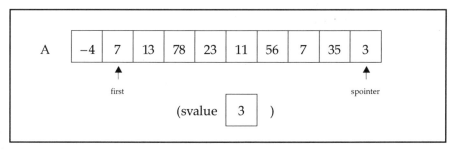

Figure 2.29 Internal sort (6)

This time the smallest value found is 3, as indicated. Exchange it with the value of the "first" element, and move first on as before; Figure 2.30.

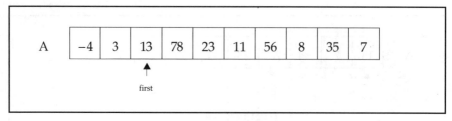

Figure 2.30   Internal sort (7)

Repeat until first is pointing to the last but one element of the array, Figure 2.31.

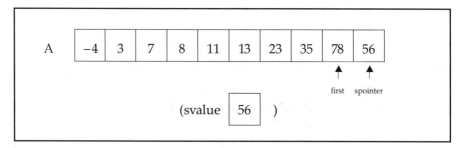

Figure 2.31   Internal sort (8)

After the last exchange, we have completely sorted the array and the process ends.

You may note that, since svalue holds the value of the smallest element after the search, we could dispense with temp and exchange by:

>A(spointer) ← A(first);
>A(first) ← svalue;

This gives a slight saving of time without adding too much obscurity.

The above process will always sort the array A into ascending order of element value. To effect a descending order sort, the "sense" of the comparison should be changed; however, the program would be more readable if the names of the variables svalue and spointer became lvalue and lpointer respectively.

Also note that, if the first element is the smallest, no exchange takes place – it would not be necessary. Note too that other methods may be more appropriate in certain cases: if, for example, the data is already partly in order. One such alternative you may wish to explore is the bubble sort; here pairs of values are compared (first with second, then second with third, then third with fourth, and so on), and the elements of the pairs are exchanged if they are in the wrong order. This way, the smallest value moves up one position at each iteration through the table – and after one iteration, the largest value is at the end.

Another alternative is to build a second array, of pointers only, so that only the pointers to the table move. At the end of the sort, that second array then becomes the index to access the table – or the table can be recreated in sequence.

You can explore other alternatives by looking at the sort phase of an external (utility) sort – this may be complex, but is usually very efficient in taking advantage of pre-sorting.

NOW TRY THESE . . .

Exercise One

a) identify each of the following data types:
       2.3, FRED, "Fred", 7, 3+4, 6.2E100

b) evaluate these expressions:

  1) (2+3*6)/2 + 4 * 3

  2) 2 < 6 AND 3 < 1

  3) PERSON + " IS " + STATUS
      where PERSON is a variable containing the character string "John",
      and STATUS is a variable containing the character string "older"

  4) NOT 4 > 7

  5) 4 < 3 AND NOT 2 > 4

Exercise Two

1) Produce the data structure for the following file:
       STUDENT-DETAILS

   Each main record contains student details and is followed by as many trailer records as the student has assignments that are complete:

main record	trailer record(s)
student number	assignment number
student name	marks
student address	grade
no. of assignments due	

2) Using the address books example, what additions would you need to make to show that:

   a) some records don't have a telephone number on file?

   b) either initials or a first name are held as well as the surname?

Exercise Three

Define the sturcture of the following record, and specify the variation of the array index:

the record contains details of the student code number, followed by the mark then the grade for each of the six assignments that the student has to complete during the year; for example:

Student Number	Assignment 1		Assignment 2		Assignment 6	
	Mark	Grade	Mark	Grade	Mark	Grade
001	40	3	60	2	45	3
002	43	3	73	1	55	2
003	56	2	75	1	53	2

3 Programming

OBJECTIVES

When you have worked through this chapter, you should be able to:

- appreciate the need for the production of robust and reliable softwaɪ
- state and explain the seven aspects of program quality
- explain the value of structured programming
- describe the process of top-down, stepwise modular programming
- describe and compare pseudocode, structure charts, structured flowcharts, decision tables and Nassi-Shneiderman diagrams, as methods of specifying an algorithm
- produce algorithms in any of these forms.

3.1 RELIABILITY AND ROBUSTNESS

Today there is more and more emphasis on computerising systems, ranging from large businesses down to the control of children's toys. System reliability is clearly important whatever the application. It can be annoying when something goes wrong with a computer controlled washing machine or an electronic till at the supermarket, however it is potentially disastrous if an air traffic control system fails or there are serious errors in an aircraft flight control system or missile guidance system. Reliability in these cases is considered to be critical and the greatest efforts have to be made to ensure that it is error free. Unfortunately no software can be tested to the point where it is considered to be absolutely correct and there will always be some residual faults. To allow for these the software not only has to be reliable, but equally important it must also be robust. Robustness is the tolerance to errors that has been deliberately built into the program. The difficulty with actually implementing checks on unspecified errors is that the potential for errors in any system is so large that for all practical purposes it can be regarded as infinite. The most effective use of finite resources therefore is to concentrate on predicting the most likely types of error, usually from past experience and an assessment of which program areas are most vulnerable, and to minimise the damage that these can do. The methods used ensure that should a fault occur the system will take the necessary action to cope in an organised and systematic manner; the comprise:

- fault detection
- damaged confinement and assessment
- recovery
- fault treatment and continued service

3.2 WHAT IS A GOOD PROGRAM?

We cannot appreciate the merits of the various approaches to programming without some understanding of the qualities needed in a program; this is because each method tries in its own way to put into practice those qualities its designers thought most important.

A "good" program has the characteristics shown below.

Accuracy	The program must do what it is supposed to do, and meet the criteria laid down in its specification.
Reliability	The program must ALWAYS do what is supposed to do, and never crash.
Efficiency	The program must use the available store space and resources in such a way that the system's speed is not wasted.
Robustness	The program should cope with invalid data without stopping with no indication as to the cause and without creating errors.
Usability	The program must be easy to use and well documented.
Maintainability	The program must be easy to amend, having good structuring and documentation.
Readability	The code in the program must be well laid out and explained with comments.

Ideally, a program should show all these – realistically this is unlikely as some of the elements are mutually exclusive. For instance, a program cannot be readable (by having the clearest logical constructs, meaningful data names and comments) **and** use the computer's memory in the most efficient way (which involves its having the most elegant, but incomprehensible, logical constructs,.

In practice, the qualities operate on a set of sliding scales, depending on the type of application; for instance, the real time programmer would put efficiency before understandability if his program were to go on a chip to control a washing machine – because of the limited space available for storing program instructions and data, and the unlikelihood of the program's needing to be changed. A payroll programmer, on the other hand, would put more emphasis on understandability rather than efficiency – first, because the computers used for his programs would have virtually unlimited storage space, and, second, because it is very likely that a payroll program would need frequent alterations in response to changes in pay rates, bonus calculations and government policy.

Making "spaghetti"

Though this book is a guide to good programming techniques, it is worth illustrating bad methods so that you know what to avoid, but first, we need a bit of history.

Computer programming began on a large scale in the 1960s. Computers themselves were new and used on a much smaller scale than today. They were physically huge but extremely limited in how much information they could hold and process. For this reason the first programmers tended to work at the same level as the machine, at what we call low level. They manipulated the electronics directly, using techniques which were the most efficient and effective for doing this.

As the scale and scope of programs grew, people used the same techniques in circumstances for which they were no longer appropriate. For instance, the logical structure needed for a machine code program to change a value in a storage cell was not the same as that for a high level commercial program controlling and recording the distribution of vehicle spares. It became obvious by the mid-1970s that we needed new concepts to deal with the shortcomings of traditional programming methods. By this time, however, vast sums of money had been invested in computers; as a result, the basic building blocks of programs, the languages, had to stay the same to protect this investment – emphasis was placed on the structuring of the programs instead.

The original linear structure of programs is the result of the von Neumann computer architecture. This hardware limitation means that programs must consist of a sequence of individual instructions, which are executed one after another. This determined how programs were first built, effectively leaving them unstructured and making them difficult to undestand. However as time went on, people found that much more of the cost of the total program was due to the cost of maintenance (as much as 80% of total) rather than that of their design and coding.

By this time, programs had been written that contained many thousands, if not millions, of instructions. The unstructured nature of these programs made their maintenance a nightmare – they cost vast amounts of money to amend, and gobbled up a vast amount of resources. Thus not enough money or resources was available for their replacement or for the development of new systems, and there was a software crisis.

Although structured programming had been developed in the 1960s by Niklaus Wirth, people still debated its benefits at the start of the 1980s, and its use is only becoming widespread now. However, as programs became longer, the lack of structuring showed in the form of spaghetti code (highly tangled) that was difficult to understand and impossible to maintain. It became clear that the benefits of structured code outweighed any disadvantages.

Why structure?

Structuring a program helps to break it down into understandable chunks. Psychologists believe that the human brain can cope with only a limited number of activities at once. Structured design cannot reduce the overall complexity of a system – but breaking it down into smaller chunks (or modules) means that the amount of detail that the programmer has to understand for any one module is much less than if dealing with the system as a whole. The job of changing (or "maintaining") the program becomes easier, and, as there is less to understand, changes can be made more quickly than if the program consists of one long continuous mixed-up piece of code.

Designing the program as a set of independent modules also allows for the following aspects:

Modular advantages

a)   We can re-use modules which contain standard procedures throughout the program, saving development time.

b)   The checking of conditions and error situations are undivided in the modules which contain the relevant coding – ensuring consistency and completeness.

c)   Testing of individual modules, in isolation, makes tracing mistakes easier.

d)   Amendments to single modules do not affect the rest of the program.

e)   We can created a library of often-used routines, which are reliable and can go in other programs.

f)   We can name modules in such a way that they are easy to find in the documentation, and consistent.

As well as making programs easier to maintain, structuring them as modules also helps create the other features of a "good program" discussed earlier.

3.3 FROM THE TOP DOWN

To achieve more of those qualities, we "abstract" programs in a structured way from the real life problems to which they relate. Abstraction simply means converting the problem from real world terms into something that we can model and solve on a computer. The first stage in this process is to adopt the correct approach for developing the program from the information available. Fortunately for today's programmers, there are many tried and tested methods. The best known of these is the top down approach.

Using this, we first look at the program as a whole, then sub-divide it into simpler components at lower levels, and repeat until no further breakdown is possible. The result is a hierarchy (upside down tree) of distinct, manageable components, whose relationships and levels are clear and simple to see.

To describe the program at its highest level, we use something called the "universal program", then by a process of "stepwise refinement" work out the details of each part of the program.

The universal program

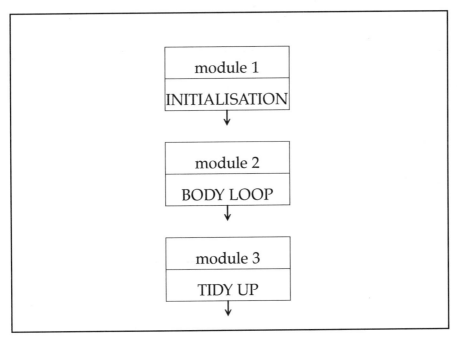

Figure 3.1   The universal program

Every working program contains a sequence of three modules (see Figure 3.1.). They are:

a) the initialisation (setting up) of all parameters (declarations and such)

b) the loop which forms the main body of the program

c) all the tidying up procedures.

The initialisation stage could involve opening files, printing headings and storing initial values, while the tidying up might include producing final summaries and totals, and closing files. The tasks to be repeated go in the central loop, which uses some special condition to finish.

This structure, used consistently, provides a reminder of each step that needs completing.

Stepwise refinement

This involves refining each module in turn, to produce a set of instructions closer and closer to those of the program language used.

For example, we could refine a step which might appear at the highest level as in Figure 3.2 to show detail as in Figure 3.3. This explains in more detail exactly what needs to be output.

OUTPUT RESULTS

Figure 3.2   Highest level step

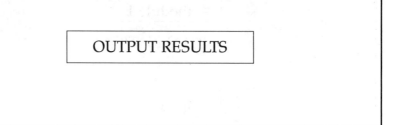

Figure 3.3   Highest level step, refined

For example

In the following example, I'll develop a program to read in a file consisting of a set of records, each of which contains a number. The processing must produce a count of the records, the sum of all the numbers and their average (sum divided by the number of records). Although this relatively simple example does not need an elaborate design process, it illustrates how the system works and how easy it is to apply to more complex design problems.

Using our universal program gives the three basic modules in diagram form as in Figure 3.4.

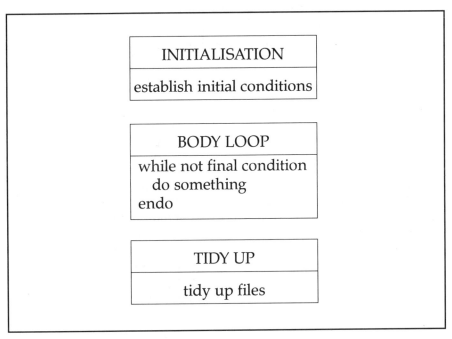

Figure 3.4   Example process

The principle of the system is that we can refine any step as much as we want, and do so when we want. To start with, we usually give the step a label (name), then break it down into its parts. The thing to avoid is going too far, too fast. We must check each step in each module against corresponding steps in other modules in order to ensure consistency. However, we have to start somewhere, so we begin by determining what the program is expected to do. At the end, we expect to have the sum of the numbers, a count of the records, and a calculation of the average, all of which we will print. So the last module would look something like Figure 3.5.

```
                    ┌─────────────────────────────┐
                    │ TIDY UP                     │
                    ├─────────────────────────────┤
                    │ print count of numbers;     │
                    │ print sum of numbers;       │
                    │ calculate average;          │
                    │ print average;              │
                    │ stop;                       │
                    └─────────────────────────────┘
```

Figure 3.5   Tidy up module

This means the program must count and add the numbers somewhere else, in order that the calculation of the mean and the printing can appear in the final module. So we must declare the variables for the count and the sum earlier in the program. In addition, we produce a definition of these and any other variables used in the program and store the details in the "data dictionary". This gives us one place where we can compare all the variables used so that there is no duplication; it also ensures that the program uses all the variables defined. (This is particularly important later when we come to test the program.) Each variable would have an entry like the example in Figure 3.6. Eventually, our program looks like Figure 3.7.

Object Name	: STD-VAT-RATE
Object Type	: Real Number
Meaning	: The standard VAT rate, as a percentage
Range	: 0 to 99
Initial Value	: 15
Where referred to	: line 1067 in INVOICING program
Where changed	: line 882 in HOUSEKEEPING program

Figure 3.6   Illustration of data dictionary entries

```
┌─────────────────────────────────────┐
│  INITIALISATION                      │
│  ├──────────────────────────────────┤
│  │ establish initial conditions;    │
│  └──────────────────────────────────┘
│
│  ┌──────────────────────────────────┐
│  │ BODY LOOP                        │
│  ├──────────────────────────────────┤
│  │ while not final condition        │
│  │    do something;                 │
│  │ endo;                            │
│  └──────────────────────────────────┘
│
│  ┌──────────────────────────────────┐
│  │ TIDY UP                          │
│  ├──────────────────────────────────┤
│  │ print count of numbers;          │
│  │ print sum of numbers;            │
│  │ calculate average;               │
│  │ print average;                   │
│  │ stop;                            │
│  └──────────────────────────────────┘
└─────────────────────────────────────┘
```

Figure 3.7   The program so far

Further refinement

Next let us think about the loop (main) module. When we set up the actual loop, it is essential to define the termination condition correctly. A common result of an inaccurately defined condition is a program with an endless loop, which would (of course) not be correct.

In the loop we define the process which will generate the required results. In its least refined form, this process is:

> obtain-number-from-file;
>
> process-number;

The condition for ending the loop is reading the last record. We can express this in a WHILE loop as:

> WHILE NOT end-of-file

Putting these together gives this loop module:

WHILE NOT end-of-file

DO

    obtain-number-from-file;

    process-number;

ENDO;

Let's give it a label, too: main-loop.

Thinking more deeply about the actions involved shows we should replace obtain-number-from-file by a READ of the file – otherwise we will keep on reading the same record! However, with a WHILE condition, it is normal to split the reads so that the program reads the first record in the file before entering the loop; after that, the remaining records in the file are read inside the loop. Thus, the main loop diagram now looks like Figure 3.8.

```
MAIN LOOP
────────────
obtain number from file;              _ _ _ _ first read
while not at end of file
   do
      process number;
      obtain number from file;        _ _ _ _ rest of reads
   endo;
```

Figure 3.8   Main-loop — refined

Now let's look at process-number. This can go into two steps, as Figure 3.9 shows.

```
PROCESS NUMBER
────────────
count of numbers ← count of numbers + 1;
sum of numbers ← sum of numbers +
                              next number;
```

Figure 3.9   Process-number – refined

If there were more processes than process-number, we could treat these in the same way – initially as labels, then boken down into their component parts.

Our program now looks like Figure 3.10; Figure 3.11 shows the breakdown of calculate-average.

INITIALISATION

establish initial conditions;

MAIN LOOP

obtain number from file
while not at end of file
  do
      count of numbers ⬅ count of numbers
      +1;
      sum of numbers ⬅ sum of numbers +
                            next number;
      obtain number from file;
  endo;

TIDY UP

print count of numbers;
print sum of numbers;
calculate average;
print average;
stop;

Figure 3.10   The developing program

CALCULATE AVERAGE

average ⬅ sum of numbers/count of numbers;

Figure 3.11   Calculate average

This decomposition (breaking down into steps) creates something of a problem for us. Our program works in most situations, but one which we haven't considered is when the loop is not entered because there are no records on file, and hence no values. The default values a language gives to declared variables depends to some extent on the language – but to be on the safe side, it is wise to give initial values of zero to each variable, as follows:

> SET count-of-numbers to 0;
>
> SET sum-of-numbers to 0;

Now, if we work out the average when count-of-numbers is 0, the result may be a problem – some languages do not allow division by 0 (as anything divided by zero is infinity!). We therefore have to introduce a check to guard against this.

In the final version of the code, the formula to calculate the average is applied only if count-of-records, ie the number of records, is more than 0. And there it is, in Figure 3.12.

```
INITIALISATION
set count of numbers to zero;
set sum of numbers to zero;

MAIN LOOP
obtain number from file;
while not at end of file
  do
    count of numbers ← count of numbers + 1;
    sum of numbers ← sum of numbers + next
    number;
    obtain number from file;
  endo;

TIDY UP
print count of numbers
if count of numbers <>0
  then
    average ← sum of numbers/count of numbers;
  else
    average ← 0;
endif;
print average;
stop;
```

Figure 3.12   Final version

3.4 BEING LOGICAL

We have reached the final program design and checked it for consistency and correctness without any thought for the final implementation. The pseudocode sequence (we call it an algorithm) is language independent – we can now code in almost any language with structures equivalent to those in the pseudocode.

The programmer often receives the program specification in pseudocode; however, there are a number of other ways to express problem logic: structure diagrams, structured flowcharts and Nassi-Shneiderman charts; decision tables may also be used where there is to be a number of conditional actions. Next we look at each of those methods forms in turn.

Structure diagrams

The logical structures of a program – sequence, selection and iteration – appear on a structure chart in much the same way as we described data in Chapter 2. Thus a sequence of processes is shown as in Figure 3.13.

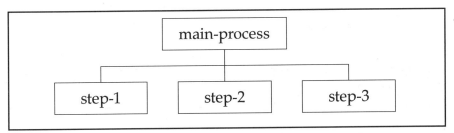

Figure 3.13   Structure diagram – sequence

Either the label for the process, or the pseudocode itself, can go into each process box, and we read these from left to right, while the hierarchy of levels is from top down. In the case of our example, main-process consists of the sub-processes step-1, step-2, and step-3 in turn.

We show selection by drawing a box for each option and putting a small circle in the top right-hand corner of each. Again, the boxes can contain either the label or the pseudocode. In this example (Figure 3.14), the choice is between type-A, type-B, and type-C.

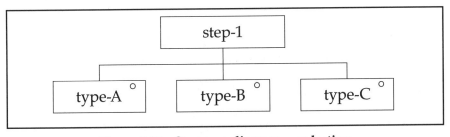

Figure 3.14   Structure diagram – selection

We also show iteration by a rectangle, this time with a star in the top right-hand corner as in Figure 3.15.

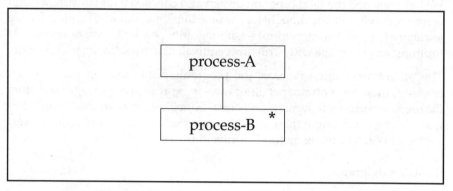

Figure 3.15   Structure diagram – iteration

In this example, process-B may repeat many times. Sometimes, if there is pseudocode in the box, we include the condition for termination.

Let us look at some more examples.

In Figure 3.16, the module for initialisation expands to three steps. Reading from left to right, the program first opens the file, then prints the main heading, and, finally, sets sum to 0.

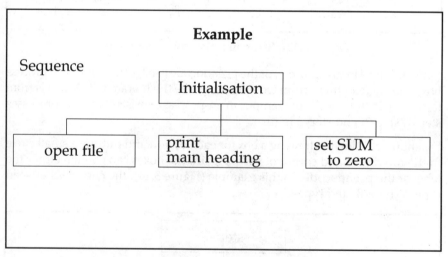

Figure 3.16   Module expanded to three steps

Figure 3.17 gives an example of selection. Customers can be processed in one of three different ways depending on the type of customer. The circle in each box indicates that one of the three modules would be executed, but not more than one.

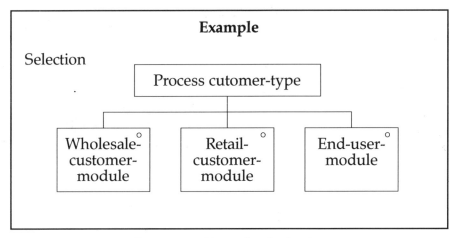

Figure 3.17 Example of selection

Figure 3.18 shows iteration. There are three sub-modules in the tax-process module, each of which is processeed in turn. However, within the process file module, the process record action will be repeated several times. We can make the loop termination more explicit by writing "process file until eof". ("eof" is a common symbol for end-of-file.) In one iteration, a pay record will first be read, then the tax calculated and the details printed. The whole process then repeats.

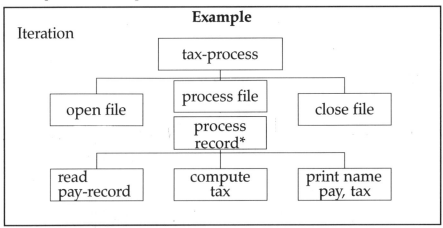

Figure 3.18   Iteration

Reading the structure diagram of Figure 3.19 from left to right, we see three modules defined at the first level expansion. Initialisation is followed by processing until eof, then the termination procedures. Expanding each module further, initialisation consists of opening the file, initialising parameters and reading one record. The three sub-modules for processing all repeat until eof – they are at a lower level than the starred box. Finally, termination consists of the conditional calculation of the mean, various prints, and closing the files.

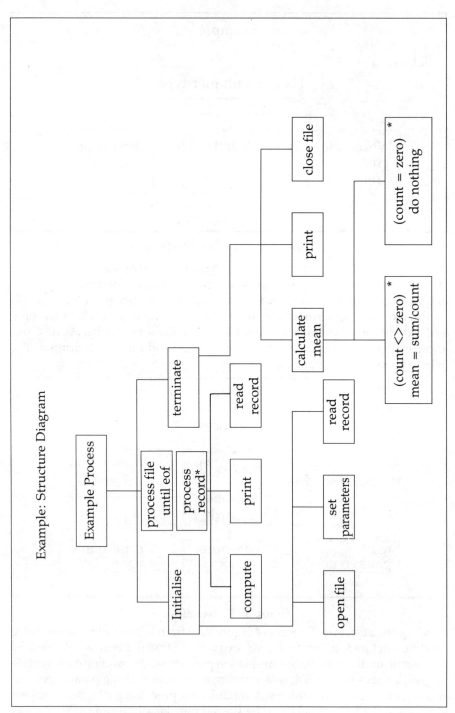

Figure 3.19 Structure diagram

Comparing these structure diagrams with the examples of data structure charts in Chapter 2 shows how easy it is to derive a logical program structure from a description of the data in structured form. Indeed, this is the underlying principle behind the "Jackson" structured programming method; this uses a description of the records and fields as the basis for the program logic.

Structured flowcharts

Flowcharts were the first tools developed for design. The more modern structured flowcharts add the concepts of hierarchies and of modules with single entry and exit points. Though many people feel flowcharts are not suited to logic design, as they are rather inflexible, they are still common for describing the logic of a process or system once the design is fixed. Indeed software is available to produce a flowchart from a source program; if you have such a program available, it represents in many ways the most satisfactory solution. However, as a programmer you would certainly have to produce flowcharts sometimes – ensure you make a good job of it by using the best set of standards.

We can construct most procedural flowcharts using a very small set of standard symbols, fully described in the NCC *Data Processing Documentation Standards* manual. The two most important are the symbols for process and for decision. In addition, there is a terminal symbol and, if need be, a connector. See Figure 3.20.

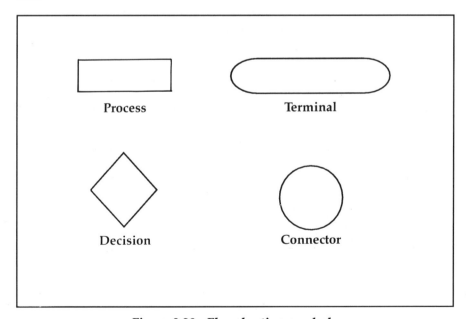

Figure 3.20   Flowcharting symbols

These symbols will never appear on a flowchart without some annotation written inside them. Figure 3.21 shows what I mean.

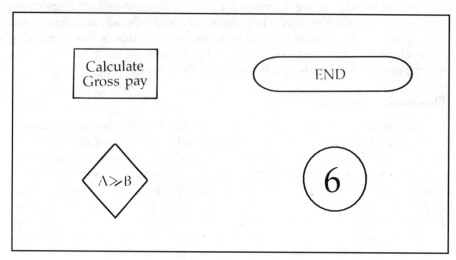

Figure 3.21   Symbol annotation

The size of the symbols is never important — draw as small as possible while keeping annotation clear. The best way to ensure neat flowcharts is to make use of a standard template (metal or plastic sheet with cut out holes, such as the one available from NCC).

One of the problems of drawing flowcharts is flow-lines which intersect or cross. There are standards for joining flow-lines, but no solution for two lines that cross but do not join. The only sensible thing to do is to avoid it! If you design programs according to the methods described in this and earlier chapters, then a flowchart drawn from such a design will have no crossing lines. Each of the three fundamental logic elements has a completely self-contained flowchart representation, which may be easily incorporated into an overall description of a process. Let us see this in more detail.

Sequence

We can easily draw a sequence of one or more processes as in Figure 3.22. Since the standard logic flow is from top to bottom or from left to right, we need no arrow heads here (though it would not be wrong to include them if it made the chart easier to follow).

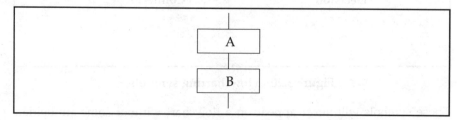

Figure 3.22   Flowchart sequence

Selection

The decision symbol shows selection as in Figure 3.23. This is equivalent to the code:

     IF test

        THEN A;

        ELSE B;

        ENDIF;

See how the flow-lines come together after the alternative processes A and B, so that the flowchart section still has a single entry and a single exit. This makes it easier to join various elements when drawing a larger flowchart.

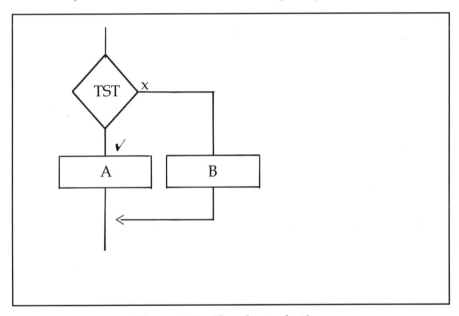

Figure 3.23   Flowchart selection

Iteration (looping)

As described earlier, there are two fundamental loop elements, the WHILE and the REPEAT. Each has its own flowchart representation: Figure 3.24. Again, in each case we have a single entry and a single exit, which makes combination simple.

When you draw a flowchart, aim for clarity by avoiding too much detail. You can achieve this by using a hierarchy of flowcharts in a series, giving more and more detail. In order to indicate that another chart describes a process in more detail, we use a system of cross-referencing: a reference to the more detailed chart goes in a strip across the top of the process symbol, as in Figure 3.25.

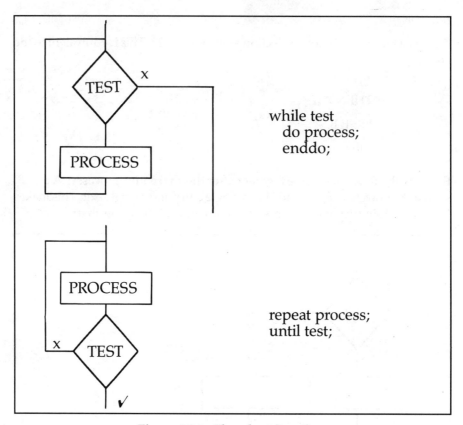

Figure 3.24   Flowchart iteration

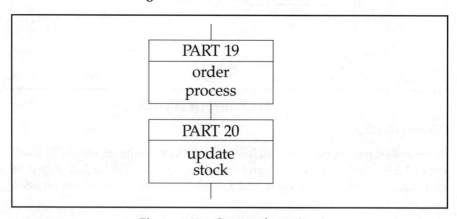

Figure 3.25   Cross-referencing

If possible, avoid the connector symbol as it makes it harder to interpret a chart. Another point to remember is that the purpose of the flowchart is to indicate the logical flow of the procedure, rather than the detail of how things are done

– this is best expressed in the programming language. Since the flowchart is for logic description rather than for design, it is quite likely that you draw it after writing the program. At all costs avoid building a flowchart by drawing boxes around program statements. This adds nothing to understanding and can also lead to confusion (especially when you include data declarations in a chart).

Decision tables

The procedural flowchart, referred to above, perhaps best suits simple, sequential processes. Although there is a symbol for indicating a selection or decision, its use will make the flowchart harder to draw and to follow. If a procedure involves a large number of related decisions, the chart becomes highly complex. For such cases, try the tabular approach developed using what we call decision tables.

A decision table is simply a table showing the various actions to be taken for different combinations of conditions. Since it specifies only the logic rules involved, and says nothing about the procedure used, a decision table is more problem oriented than a flowchart (which is solution oriented). The decision table represents a much higher level statement about a problem than does a flowchart, which relates closely to the coding sequence. As a result, decision tables are more useful than flowcharts as an aid to program design.

The four basic elements of a decision table are:

- the condition stub
- the condition entry
- the action stub
- the action entry.

The condition stub and condition entries describe the conditions to be tested, while the action stub and action entries concern the actions to be taken. In a decision table these four elements form quadrants, as in Figure 3.26.

Condition stub	Condition entries
Action stub	Action entries

Figure 3.26 Layout of a decision table

The table lists all the conditions relating to a procedure, one below another, in the condition stub; the action stub lists all possible actions. The condition entries and action entries together constitute one or more "rules", which run vertically through the two right-hand quadrants. Each rule indicates the actions needed when a particular set of conditions applies.

A limited entry table gives the conditions as simple YES/NO questions, whereas in an extended entry table the conditions have more than two possible states. Similarly, in a limited entry table the only actions are "execute" or "do not execute": no such restriction applies to an extended entry table.

Look at the limited decision table in Figure 3.27. The problem is to determine the discount rate and delivery conditions for the sale of television sets. Sets come in either walnut or plastic finish, and there are two screen sizes available. In the action entries X means execute, while a dash (−) means do not execute.

TV Discount	Rule 1	Rule 2	Rule 3	Rule 4	Rule 5	Rule 6	Rule 7	Rule 8
Approved Dealer?	Y	Y	Y	Y	N	N	N	N
Walnut Finish?	Y	Y	N	N	Y	Y	N	N
23" screen?	Y	N	Y	N	Y	N	Y	N
5% Discount	−	−	−	−	X	X	X	X
20% Discount	−	−	X	X	−	−	−	−
25% Discount	X	X	−	−	−	−	−	−
Free Delivery	X	X	−	−	−	−	−	−
Cash Payment	−	−	−	−	X	X	X	−

Figure 3.27   Decision table example − limited entry

From Figure 3.27, we can see that, under the following conditions:

approved dealer?	No
walnut finish?	Yes
23 inch (59cm) screen?	Yes

rule 5 will apply; the appropriate actions are:

allow 5% discount
charge for delivery
insist on payment in cash

An example of an extended entry table appears in Figure 3.28. Using this table, do you agree that an order is approved if a guarantee is available and credit is 100, or if there is no guarantee but there is special clearance? Depending upon which rule applies, further action is taken according to table A, B or C.

Order Approval	1	2	3	4
Guarantee available?	Y	N	N	N
Credit balance?	£100	£200	£100	£100
Special clearance?	–	–	Y	N
Accept order	X	X	X	–
Refer to client	–	–	–	X
Go to table	A	B	C	–

Figure 3.28 Decision table example – extended entry

Notice that in rules 1 and 2 special clearance does not apply; I show this by a blank condition entry. This reduces the table size, and is an example of the following general rule in action:

If, for any combination of two rules, the condition entries are the same except one row, and the action entries are identical, we can combine the two rules and insert a dash in place of the conditions which differ.

Simple rules			**Combined rule**
1	4		
Y	Y		Y
Y	N	Reduces	–
N	N	to	N
–	–		–
X	X		X
–	–		–
X	X		X

Figure 3.29 Combining rules

This is an important rule, as it enables us to build manageable tables even with large numbers of conditions. Remember that, in general, N conditions will lead to N^2 rules, unless we can reduce the table in such a way. So if we apply similar reductions to our earlier TVDISCOUNT table, it becomes as shown in Figure 3.30.

TV Discount	1	2	3	4
Approved Dealer?	Y	Y	N	N
Walnut Finish?	Y	N	–	N
23″ screen?	–	–	–	N
5% Discount	–	–	X	X
20% Discount	–	X	–	–
25% Discount	X	–	–	–
Free Delivery	X	–	–	–
Cash Payment	–	–	X	–

Figure 3.30   Limited entry redrawn with combined rules

Another way to simplify a decision table is to use an ELSE (otherwise) rule; in other words "if no other rules apply, use this one". The table in Figure 3.31 shows this; note that in the first version I use a combined rule. Note, too, that I leave the condition entries for the ELSE rule blank, or write the word ELSE in the entry column.

Once we have drawn up a decision table for a given problem, it is relatively easy to check that we have thought of all possible conditions, and in the right combinations.

So far, we have not considered the order in which the various actions associated with a rule are executed. If (as is often the case) this order of events is important, we can show it by replacing the Xs in the action entries with numbers indicating the order. Suppose, for example, a rule performs actions A, B, C, D, E and F, and that the following constraints apply:

do B before D and C

do C and D before A or F

do A and F before E

Version 1	1	2	3	4	5	6	7
Test A true?	Y	Y	Y	N	N	N	N
Test B true?	Y	N	N	Y	Y	N	N
Test C true?	–	Y	N	Y	N	Y	N
Goto table 2A	–	–	X	–	–	–	–
Goto table 2B	–	–	–	–	X	–	–
Goto table 2C	–	–	–	–	–	X	–
Goto Errortable	X	X	–	X	–	–	X

Reduces to:

Version 2	1	2	3	ELSE
Test A true?	Y	N	N	
Test B true?	N	Y	N	
Test C true?	N	N	Y	
Goto table 2A	X	–	–	–
Goto table 2B	–	X	–	–
Goto table 2C	–	–	X	–
Goto Errortable	–	–	–	X

or even to:

Version 3	1	2	3	
Test A true?	Y	N	N	E
Test B true?	N	Y	N	L S
Test C true?	N	N	Y	E
Goto Table	2A	2B	2C	Error

Figure 3.31 Table reduction – ELSE rule

Then we can mark the actions as in Figure 3.32.

Perform A	3
Perform B	1
Perform C	2
Perform D	2
Perform E	4
Perform F	3

Figure 3.32   Action sequence numbering

Of course, this numbering allows the system to carry out actions C and D in either order, even at the same time if that is possible.

Processing a decision table

Once you've built a decision table and checked it for consistency and completeness, you may convert it into a program. There are four basic methods of doing this, of implementing the table:

- coding from the table by hand
- using a pre-processor – which converts the table into a source program suited for input to a compiler
- using a program which interprets (translates) the table
- using a special compiler to translate the decision table into machine code.

The last three need suitable software, and you must stick closely to standard forms for the tables. When using manual methods, take care to test the conditions in the correct order, or you will produce an unnecessarily complicated procedure.

Nassi-Shneiderman diagrams

These diagrams are derived from an idea in 1973 by Nassi and Shneiderman for a replacement for traditional flowcharts that better suits writing structured code. They have had some success, but are often criticised as being suitable only for lower level specifications.

Here, rectangles enclosing pseudocode stand for the procedures, and we read from the top of the diagram to the bottom. Figure 3.33 shows a simple sequence of three actions: A, then B, then C. A WHILE loop of the same actions controlled by a condition appears as in Figure 3.34.

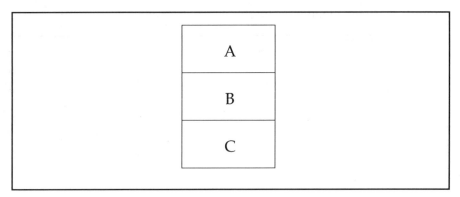

Figure 3.33   Nassi-Shneiderman sequence

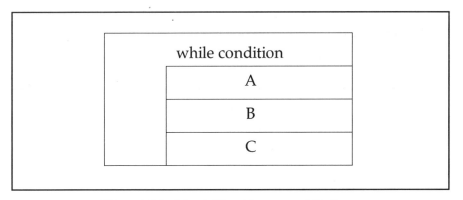

Figure 3.34   Nassi-Shneiderman while loop

Similarly, a REPEAT loop of these actions would be, in diagram form, as in Figure 3.35.

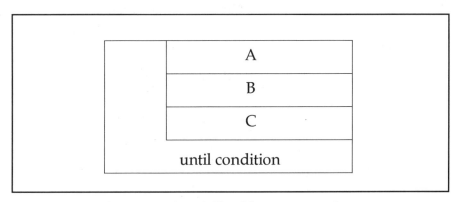

Figure 3.35   Nassi-Shneiderman repeat loop

Figure 3.36 shows a loop repeating an action indefinitely.

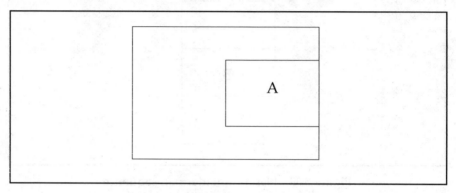

Figure 3.36   Nassi-Shneiderman indefinite loop

We show selection by dividing the rectangle into parts, one part with the condition and the rest the range of possible values: Figure 3.37. In this example, if the result of testing the condition is true (T), we use procA; if false (F) procB follows.

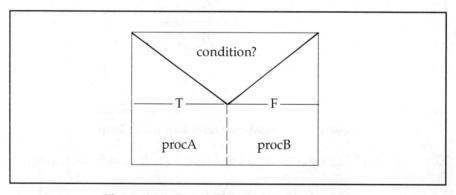

Figure 3.37   Nassi-Shneiderman selection

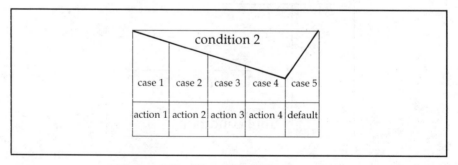

Figure 3.38   Nassi-Shneiderman case

For a CASE construct, the rectangle is divided into more parts, Figure 3.38. The procedure followed would depend on the value of the condition.

Finally, these diagrams can also show actions which might take place together. Currently only one high level computer language Ada – supports concurrency, as this is called. Figure 3.39 gives the diagram for this. It shows that after the process A actions, we can have process B1, process B2 and process B3 taking place concurrently, followed by process C.

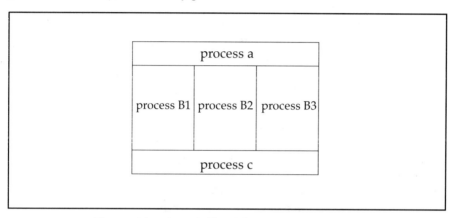

Figure 3.39   Nassi-Shneiderman concurrency

The next example, Figure 3.40, shows a full program design. The program starts with an initialisation process. Then it checks for the end of the file; if this is the case, it enters the termination routine via the left-hand branch: otherwise it tests the record to see whether it is type 1 or 2. If it is type 1, it follows process 1 then process 3; if it is type 2 it goes through process 2, then through process 3. The program repeats this until it reaches the end of the file, at which point it moves to the termination process.

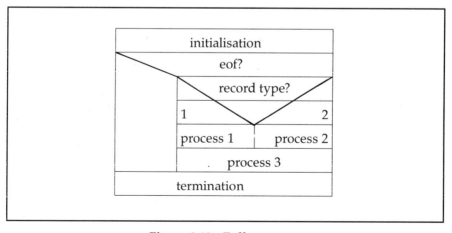

Figure 3.40   Full program

3.5 COMPARING THE METHODS

You can get some idea of the differences and similarities between the various methods of logic description by thinking about the following descriptions of the same process. First, here's the process in pseudocode.

master-file update:
   WHILE more-transactions or more-master-records
    DO
     IF master-key = transaction-key
      THEN update master-record from transaction-record;

       WRITE updated master-record;
       GET next valid transaction-record;
       GET next master-record;
      ELSE
       IF master-key < transaction-key
       THEN WRITE master-record;
       GET next master-record;
       ELSE
       PRINT error-message;
       GET next valid transaction-record
     ENDIF;
    ENDO;
   CLOSE transaction-file;
   CLOSE master-file;

The approach used usually depends on installation standards or on the programmer's familiarity with a particular method.

Pseudocode is nearest to program languages and therefore easy to code from. Loop and selection structures are straightforward and clear. You can show levels and there is a certain freedom of expression. It is easy to learn and to produce quickly. You can also use it as an intermediate step when design charts are not easy to code. However, it does not have the pictorial property of some of the other methods; therefore, levels and relationships are not so obvious.

The flowchart was the first tool developed to express logic design and is closest to human thinking. It was found to have several drawbacks, however, especially in handling iteration and selection. As program languages developed, people found they could not code directly from the flowchart structures and they seemed clumsy to use. The structured flowchart overcomes some of these problems and is also diagrammatic.

In many ways structure diagrams are a good solution when there are complex programs consisting of many modules. Levels and relationships are clear and you can see the problem at a glance. These diagrams do not show loop structures explicitly, but we can reduce this drawback by writing some form of pseudocode in the boxes.

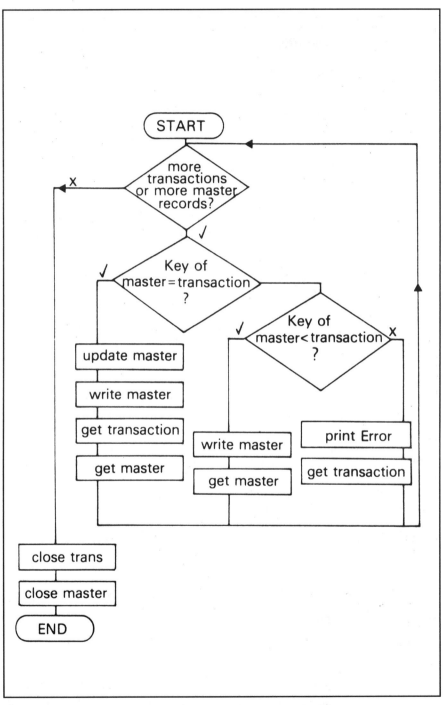

Figure 3.41　Illustration in flowchart form

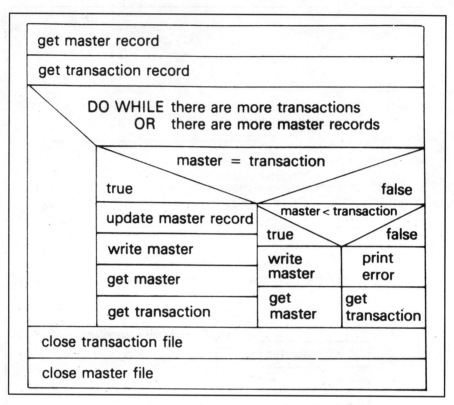

Figure 3.42 Illustration as Nassi-Shneiderman diagram

Nassi-Shneiderman charts make the scope of the different structures and of different variables very clear, and translate very easily into structured programs. However the drawings can grow with the design. A good diagram can be made only after the overview of the whole program is available. Changes usually mean re-drawing the complete chart.

NOW TRY THESE . . .

Exercise One

From the details supplied construct an appropriate set of decision tables.

THE PROGRAM SPECIFICATION

PROJECT

1. The Company and Products
    MKC Limited manufacture items of domestic furniture. Currently they make four different products, M1 to M4. Each can be made in one of three finishes, teak (T), white (W) and rosewood (R). The teak and

rosewood versions can be "antiqued" (TA and RA). Example product codes M1W, M4RA.

MKC make to order — with despatch objectives of ten working days from receipt of order for a single unit. Large orders take longer. All parts are issued to manufacture in same week as order received. The company has installed a microcomputer with a standard package covering invoicing, ledgers and stock recording.

A new system is required to assist purchasing and stock control. Two parts files will be maintained, one as a "product breakdown", the other as a "used-on" record.

Parts are given a non-meaningful five-digit number, in the stock recording system. Sub-assemblies of parts are given four-digit numbers; again, non-meaningful. A product is made of (up to) 15 sub-assemblies. Sub-assemblies are made from between two and five different parts. Parts are stocked — sub-assemblies are not stocked — and final assembly is done by the customer on receipt. The manufacturing process therefore consists only of making sub-assemblies from parts. The despatch department packs appropriate quantities of each sub-assembly in cartons — one carton for one product.

2.   Stock File: (already existing — contains other fields, but these are the relevant ones)

Main Record: Part No: Description (up to 30 chars)
Quantity in stores
Minimum re-order quantity
Delivery lead time (weeks) (Note: currently 6 weeks maximum)
Flag indicating "development part — not used in production"

Trailer Records: Order number
Order quantity
Order week number

(There are as many trailer records for a part as there are outstanding orders for that part.)

3.   Product Breakdown

The records are required to be grouped as follows:

Type 1   Product Code
Sub-assembly number*
Quantity off*

(*This pair of fields repeated up to 15 times)

Type 2   Sub-assembly number
Part number*
Quantity off*
(*This pair of fields repeated up to 15 times)

A single type-1 record is followed by up to 15 type-2 records, then another type-1 and so on. Currently there are 20 products, but more may be added. Where a sub-assembly is used on more than one product, its constituents will be repeated in a separate type-2 record for each product. (There are very few such cases.)

4.   Used-on File

This file will be created from the Product Breakdown file, and will be re-created automatically from that file whenever the Product Breakdown is updated in any way.
It contains one record for each part number, as follows:
Part Number
Product Code*
Quantity used*
(*This pair of fields repeated for each Product on which the part number is used)

5.   The Program to be Designed

The program allows the input of future estimated orders, and shows the effect that this would have on stocks. It can also be used to input known orders and to trigger any necessary orders for parts.

5.1   Input stage

Current week number will be input, and the quantities of each Product forecast for that week (currently up to 20 Products). The information will be repeated for each of the succeeding nine weeks.

5.2   Process

The program will then use that matrix of ten weeks by 20 Products (may grow beyond 20) to build up a pattern of demand for each part, one by one, and will compare the demand with the stock available and on order (assuming expected deliveries are made).

5.3   Output

For each part, an appropriate demand pattern will be displayed or printed, together with a latest order date (which may be earlier than the current week number) to avoid running out of stock. The total quantity required will be shown, and the minimum order quantity will also be provided for reference. The value of each order signalled will be calculated, and the total order value for each week displayed at the end of the run.

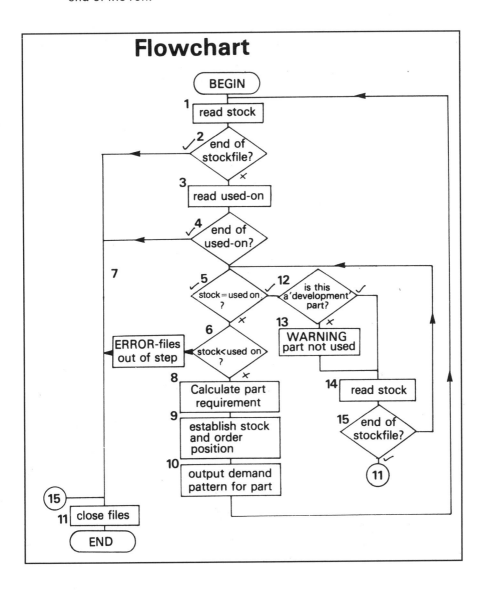

4   The design process

OBJECTIVES

When you have worked through this chapter, you should be able to:

- describe in detail the nature of a program specification
- describe and use structured English as a method of program specification
- distinguish between the four main logical types of data file
- explain the need for, and the techniques of, file searching, creation, amendment and deletion
- describe principles, and explain methods, of formatting output on screen and on paper
- explain the need to check program design
- outline and compare dry running and the walk-through as methods of program design checking.

INTRODUCTION

We have now looked at three major aspects of the process of producing a program – the main program and data structures, and the meaning of program quality in relation to design.

Before we turn to the actual processes of coding, we need to see something more of the design stage: the crucial first step of program development. In particular, we consider program specification and checking, and go into more depth on file structure.

4.1   THE PROGRAM SPECIFICATION

The starting point for the design of any computer program must be a proper specification of its intended behaviour. It is most usual to describe this behaviour pattern in terms of the necessary inputs and the required outputs. The programmer's problem is then to design a process (or algorithm) which will, given the correct inputs, derive from them the required outputs. In addition to the descriptions of these inputs and outputs, a program specification may include a description of any constraints which must apply to the solution. These may include details of run time and/or space limitations, available equipment and utilities, as well as project deadlines.

Within a program specification, the definitions of the inputs and outputs must include a description of their meaning, so that the programmer can understand the relationship between them.

For instance, one may need a program to find the area of a triangle given the lengths of its three sides. Such a statement of the problem is almost a complete specification – the programmer needs to know only the properties of triangles in order to handle it. (You can always refer to a text book if stuck!) The problem as stated has meaning only because we understand the terms "triangle", "area" and "side", and their inter-relationships. If, on the other hand, the specification is "given x, y and z, compute A", it would be meaningless without a definition of A, x, y and z.

Any program written in a business environment is part of a software system to carry out a certain processing task. An actual data processing package would consist of a large number of programs, each handling one activity. For example, in a software package used by a sales department, one program may enter daily sales into data files. Another program uses the records on these data files to produce a particular report.

The specification in Figure 4.1 raises many unanswered questions: see Figure 4.2.

> ### Given the daily sales figures of a company, write
> ### a program to determine the total sales
> ### for a month

Figure 4.1   Specification example (insufficient)

If there are no further details, a group of twenty programmers could produce twenty different versions without any of them coming close to what the user had in mind.

A program needs to be fully specified, because it is part of a larger system and its design must be consistent with the methods used overall. In a commercial environment, the specification would come from a systems analyst, or systems manager, who studies user requirements and is responsible for the design and co-ordination of a software project. The analyst hands over the specifications to a team of programmers, each of whom works on a set of programs.

A commercial system is designed to meet the needs of the customer who will be its ultimate user. The outputs and reports, the screen messages and questions, and the inputs required – the user must understand all these and find them similar to those already in use. The users should therefore have as close a connection as possible with specifying the requirements. When they are satisfied, they will generally have to issue a formal "acceptance" of the specification, by signing relevant documents. Because the programmers may not get a chance to interact with the users themselves, they must be able to understand the specifications and follow them rigidly. Any improvements which they would like to suggest should be raised at the appropriate meetings.

How will daily sales be given?
  – on a file? Disk? Tape?
  – entered through keyboard?

What sort of figures should be expected?
  – what units?
  – what range? eg crores? lakhs?

Output is required on
  – monitor?
  – printed report?

Who is the output for?
What should it look like?
Which machine will be used?

  – many different programs possible

Figure 4.2 Some additional questions

Moreover, because he is part of a team, the programmer must document his programs in a predetermined way, so that the rest of the team can easily understand them. This sometimes means that programmers who are new to a team have the additional burden of adapting to the standards for specifications and documentation that are already in use by the team as a whole.

The scope of the specification

Most of the programs written today form part of much larger systems. To help a programmer understand a particular program's significance, its position in the entire system should be clear. Since an overall systems specification should be known before individual programs are specified, all the programmer needs to do is study the documentation. He should find, among other things, an overall system description in diagrammatic form. This may take the form of a system run chart, showing all files and programs involved – or it may be a data flow diagram, in which specific files are not mentioned. In either case the role played by the particular program under consideration should be clear.

The program gains a name according to the naming conventions in use; also, in addition to a description of the program inputs and outputs in the form of detailed record formats, the programmer will probably receive a description of the function of the program in some form.

Program function

A popular method used to describe the function of a program is structured English: this is easy to write and understand.

Structured English is a subset of the English language, consisting of a limited set of verbs and nouns organised to represent a reasonable compromise between readability and rigour. Human languages (like Hindi, French, and so on) contain complexities that make them too vague for use in program specification. Take, for example, this phrase – "calculate 8 and 2 divided by 2". It could mean add 8 to 2 then divide the result by 2, or add 8 to the result of 2 divided by 2.

The purpose of structured English is to allow the analyst to describe, rigorously and precisely, the business policy (but not the implementation tactics) for each of the processes of the system. At the same time the description should be clear to the average user. In its most extreme form, structured English consists of only the elements given below.

Elements of structured English

- a limited set of action-oriented verbs, such as "find" and "print"
- control constructs borrowed from structured programming – eg if...then...else, while...do, and so on, like the ones in our free format language
- objects defined in a data dictionary.

As an example of structured English, consider the specification listed below. It is of a manual process applied to overdue invoices.

1   If the amount of the invoice times the number of weeks overdue is greater than 5000

   a give a copy of the invoice to the salesperson who is to phone the customer

   b note on the back of the invoice that this has been done, with the date

   c refile the invoice in a file for examining again in two weeks

2   **else**

   if more than four overdue notices have been sent

   a give a copy of the invoice to the appropriate salesperson who is to phone the customer

   b record on the back of the invoice that this has been done, with the date

   c refile the invoice in the file to be examined in one week

3 else

the situation has not yet reached serious proportions, but a reminder is to be sent:

a add 1 to the overdue notice count on the back of the invoice (if there is no such count, write "overdue notice count = 1")

b if the invoice on the file is illegible, type a new one

c send the customer a copy of the invoice, stamped "Nth notice: invoice overdue. Please remit immediately", where N is the value of the overdue notice count

d record on the back of the invoice the date of the Nth overdue notice

e refile the invoice in the file for examination in two weeks

4.2 DATA STORAGE

We discussed variables, arrays and tables earlier. It is now time to take this a stage further – and consider how we store data on a permanent basis. This is done through "external" files of various types, kept on magnetic tape and/or disk; each consists of many records.

Records

It is easiest to view records as one dimensional arrays which consist of a series of related data items. They differ from one dimensional arrays in that arrays always contain elements of the same type – whereas the data items in a record can be of different types. Figure 4.3 gives an example.

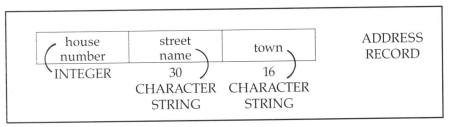

Figure 4.3 Record structure

In a record each element has its own identifier, whereas array elements are referred to by subscripts. The elements in each record are called "fields".

File types

Records live together in files. These can be one of four different types.

Serial file

Each record is written after the last record in the current file. The order of records in the serial file is according to the time when the data was generated. Examples are: memory dumps; archival files; record of events; transaction files.

Sequential file

Here records are in sequence of one or more key fields. We produce these files by sorting serial files. Examples: student marks file arranged according to the roll numbers of the students, with the key field being roll-number; transactions file arranged by customer account number, then by item number: primary key = account number, secondary key = item number.

Indexed sequential file

Instead of rearranging the entire file, an additional file is generated, storing an index like that in a book. This holds the key field from each record in sorted sequence, along with the address of the corresponding record. Such an index is useful only if we can access records directly – therefore we use this type of file only with direct access media (disks and chips). To access the file, the index file is consulted first.

Direct access file

For quick and direct access, each record goes at an address generated by applying a formula to the record key. There is no need for an index file, but space utilisation may be inefficient. The formula depends on the type of data, and should give the best use of storage space. Example: flight reservations with record address generated from the flight number.

Record and file formats

Format means lay out – so here we look at how we can organise the data in a record or file. Example formats for files and records appear in Figures 4.4 and 4.5. You can see that the file specification consists of collections of record specifications. These provide good checklists for future reference.

4.3 HANDLING FILES

In addition to being able to look at a file we also want to manipulate (process) it in different ways. Thus one has to be able to create files, change or delete the data on them, or erase an entire file. Sometimes files also have to be sorted or merged.

File operations

The methods for opening and closing a file are the same for all file types, but reading from and writing to them is different.

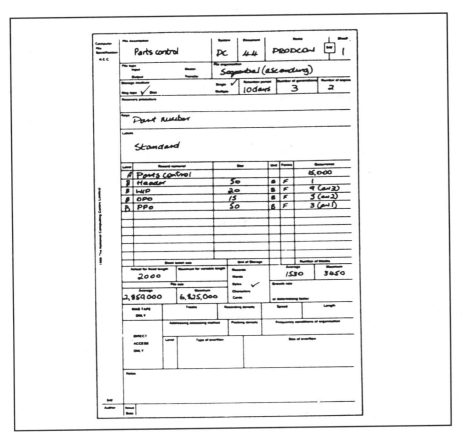

Figure 4.4   Form S42, Computer file specification

Figure 4.5   Form S44, Record specification

Reading a file

The method used to get data from a file is called the mode of access. We can access serial and sequential files only sequentially: that is one record after another. We can access indexed files both sequentially and directly. Direct access allows us to reach individual records by using an index (which relates the record key to its physical position on its storage medium).

Tape files can be accessed only serially or sequentially because of the fact that records appear one after another – so there is no other way of selecting them. The difference between the two access methods is that as serial files have no key specified, and therefore are in no particular sequence, they cannot be accessed sequentially. We discussed this in Section 2.6.

These four basic methods of organising files all apply to files on disk: serially and sequentially as for tape; indexed sequentially – the records have keys as with a sequential file, but in addition have a separate index linking the key with its disk address; directly – the records go on disk using a formula to relate the key value to the actual storage address.

Serial and sequential files can be accessed only serially or sequentially, just as with tape file. Indexed sequential files can be accessed sequentially, each record being read in sequence using the index to locate the physical position – or directly, where records aren't read as an ordered sequence but in a disordered way, with no sequence to the keys chosen. Direct files are usually accessed at "random", in that they need processing in no special order – and any key can directly produce the correct physical address of the record, as long as the system knows the formula.

Let's look at some specific processing examples. To search for a particular record on a serial file, each record on the file has to be read until the correct record is found. If a second record is needed, we have to go back to the beginning of the file and start again. This method is adequate if all the records on the file are to be processed, and we expect no link between files. If either of these conditions is not the case, the serial file is not good enough. Then we need to work with a sequential file.

To search for a record on a sequential file the key must be specified. Beginning at the first record on the file, the key field on each record is checked. When a match is found, the record is processed. Unless the next key needed has a higher value, the file then has to be closed and reopened at the start before any checking can begin.

Indexed sequential files are created differently depending on the language. In COBOL the index is created automatically when the file is declared. Subsequently, the index is referred to whenever a record is to be accessed.

With direct (sometimes called random) files, the program uses the key of the record to work out the record address. Thus the order of keys of any queries is unimportant – each read is accomplished without any resetting of the file.

In the case of languages other than those like COBOL, it might be necessary to write the full file handling procedures to create and use an index.

Amending files

The main activities that make up file amendment are:

- adding records
- deleting them
- altering the data on them.

We can amend an indexed file by reading the appropriate record, changing the data, and then rewriting it. This is not possible with a sequential file as records can go only at the end of the file. To update a sequential file, each record has to be read, changed, then written out to a new file.

As we have to process a sequential file from start to end, any changes to it have to be in the same order. To do this all the amendment records go onto a transaction file; the system then sorts this using the same key fields as the main file. We shall look at the method used (an "external" sort) later.

When both files are in the same key order they are opened. The key of the first record to be amended comes from the transaction file, and the original file ("old master") is read in and written out record by record, until a match is found. Any changes are made and the changed record goes to the new file (the "new master"). The key of the next record is found by reading the next record on the transaction file – the process repeats until there are no more transaction file records. Then all that is required is for the rest of the old master file to go to the new file. Deletion involves simply missing out the "write" part of the process.

If a key value is on the transaction file, but there is no corresponding record on the old master, then we need an appropriate insert or error procedure.

The logic structure of a file processing program roughly corresponds to the structure of a file, with one module to process the header record, another to process the data records and a third to process the trailer record, as Figure 4.6 shows.

Process file-header;
Process file matching until end-of-both-files;
Process file-trailer;
Stop.

Figure 4.6   Basic program structure

The header and trailer modules will contain opening and closing routines for the files; in addition, the first read also takes place in the header module.

The action within the main processing module depends on whether the transaction key is less than, equal to, or greater than the key on the original file. If the transaction key is greater, the old master file record can go without change to the new one.

If the two keys are equal, a deletion or amendment can be carried out. If the transaction key is less then it does not exist on the original file and an insertion is possible.

Sequential file amendment is most often used in a batch processing environment; when magnetic tape was the main medium for storage it was the most common method of file updating.

Figure 4.7 shows the procedure. Normally, the program updates a master file through the transaction file, and creates a new master. This kind of processing is still common – but sequential disk files have replaced sequential tape files. This approach is particularly suitable for very large files, and for when the hit rate is high (that is, when most of the master file records are being updated).

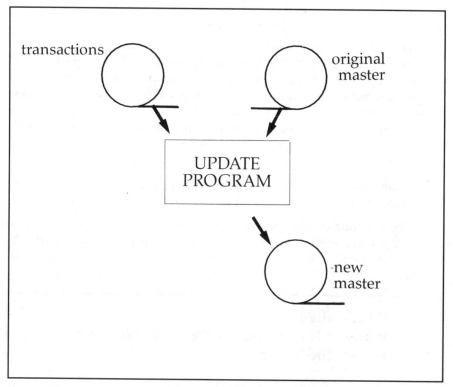

Figure 4.7   Sequential file update

In the case of indexed files, the transaction file is read to find the first record. The key of this record is used to check the index of the master file. When the program finds the master file record, it updates and rewrites it. If the corresponding master record does not exist, the transaction file record is an insertion; then the program must update the index as well as the data file. In some languages, such as COBOL, this is done automatically; in others the changes have to be coded by the programmer.

The pseudocode for an indexed sequential file update looks like that in Figure 4.8. The effect of updating is to overwrite the master file record with new data. We call this method "updating in place".

```
                         File Amendment
                            –  Indexed Files
        Control Routine
           Process File Headers;
           Process File Amends
               until end of Transaction file;
           Process File Ends;

        File Headers Routine
           Open files;
           Read Transaction file;

        File Amends Routine
           If Insert
             then
               process insert;
             else if delete
                   then
                      process delete;
                   else
                      process amendment;
           endif;
           read transaction file;

        File Ends Routine
           Close files;
```

```
        Insert Routine
           Read main file;
           if key in main file
             then
                process insert error;
             else
                write Main record
                      (file + index entry);
           endif;

        Delete Routine
           Read main file;
           if key found in main file
             then
                delete Main record;
             else
                process delete error;
           endif;

        Amends Routine
           Read main file;
           if key in main file
             then
                rewrite changed main record;
             else
                process amends error;
           endif;
```

Figure 4.8   Indexed file amendment

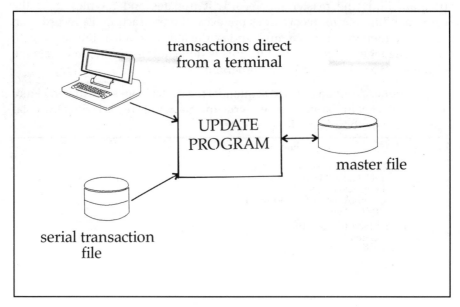

Figure 4.9   Updating in place

As the individual records of indexed sequential files are addressable, there is no need for the transaction file to be sorted. So updates can take place using either a serial file containing collected amendments, or directly from a terminal. Besides being more flexible, this avoids the extra processing we need with tape.

Though there is no index, direct files have the same advantage, in terms of being able to access individual records, as indexed sequential files. In fact, for large files and in situations where cutting access time is important, they can provide a faster alternative as it is not necessary to search the index for the record address. In terms of processing, however, the procedures for the coding are just the same.

4.4   SORTS AND MERGES

Sorting is the process of arranging items in a desired sequence. It is generally accepted that between 30% and 40% of computer time in commercial applications is spent on sorting files. Obviously it makes sense therefore to have available a general sort utility which will enable any file to be sorted, using any specified field or fields as the sequence key(s).

For example, it may be necessary to process outstanding accounts in order of invoice number, so as to match records with a particular master file; in this case the invoice number field would be the sort key. Later it may be necessary to extract customer information, such as name and address or credit limit, from the customer master file; in that case the outstanding orders would be sorted into customer order using a different field as the sort key.

While it remains desirable to provide such a generalised sort utility, there are many reasons why it is not possible to do so. Records can be of any length and format, files can be of any size and stored on a variety of media, and so on.

Many computer manufacturers solve the problem by supplying a sort/merge generator. This is a highly parameterised program which reads in the user-specified description of the files to be sorted, and creates a tailor made sort program. It is usual for different versions of such a generator to be available for handling different file media such as magnetic tape and disk. Most sorts are applied to large files, and will involve the creation and manipulation of intermediate work files. When using a sort/merge generator, take care to ensure that sufficient work files of the appropriate kind can be on offer.

Earlier I stated that for a sequential update, the program first sorts the records in a serial transaction file in the same key order as the master file. The sort that takes place is not the same as the internal sort used for tables and arrays explained in Chapter 2 – this is an "external" sort, so called because the whole file is not read into the computer store for the sort to take place, but kept outside.

Most files are too large to fit into the store at one time, so they are sorted using a multiple pass sort/merge technique. A large number of utilities are available to do this, and generally the programmer does not have to know exactly how they work to use them. Let's look at one type to get the general idea.

Depending on the size of the store available, a section of the file (which we will call N records) is read in, sorted internally, then dumped onto an intermediate work file. Another set of records is read in, sorted, and written onto a second work file. Alternate sets are sorted and written onto the two work files until the end of the unsorted file.

Records from work files 1 and 2 are read in and output to work files 3 and 4 as merged strings, 2*N records long, in the proper sequence. In the second pass longer strings are output to files 1 and 2, and so on. Eventually each work file contains just one string. In the final phase these two are merged to form the output file.

Sort utilities try to make use of all available storage and create many temporary files depending on backup space, and the number and kind of devices available. Temporary files are erased at the end, and the sorted data is available in an output file. The more storage that is available, the faster the sort. With tape-based systems there may be up to four intermediate files; with direct access devices there are generally fewer.

4.5   OUTPUT FORMATTING

Printer and screen layouts

The length and width of the page used on the printer are standardised as part of the specification. The number of characters per line would normally vary from

80 to 160 normal sized characters (with a larger range if the size is changed). The page contains heading lines, data lines and footing lines spaced by top, bottom, right, and left margins.

The main heading, such as the name of the company, and one or more subheadings, such as the name of the report, is normally followed by a line of column headings. The main body of the report contains the detail – lines of figures filling the columns. At the end, footing lines contain such data as page totals and page numbers. Some of the headings would be repeated on every new page if the report goes to more than one page, while the footing line is generated as soon as the computer senses that a page is about to end. At the end of the report there may be special lines giving final totals and messages. See Figure 4.10.

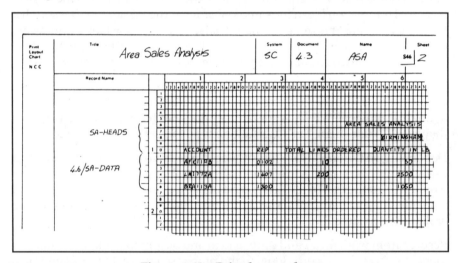

Figure 4.10 Print layout chart

To prepare a print layout chart, people use a special sheet, marked like graph paper, with a square for every print position (character space) on the printed page. The print layout is indicated on this by specifying print positions, margins, and messages.

A display screen, on the other hand, normally allows up to 24 lines with 80 characters per line. Within this area there can be headings, prompts, data lines, and error messages. Note that it may be necessary to overlay a section of the screen several times with new data within a program, without erasing the entire screen each time. A screen layout chart is similar to the print layout chart except that the number of lines is restricted to 24.

On a display screen the same area is used over and over again with screen formats of different types replacing each other, or being overlaid. When writing a program which uses the screen, take care to erase the remains of printed messages when they are no longer required.

A significant difference compared to producing a printed report is in the "scrolling" which screens offer instead of a page by page report display.

It is often a temptation for a programmer to introduce special variations into the screen display, but do not forget that using a monitor is a strain on the eyes – it is therefore important to minimise the amount of reading that the user has to do, and to avoid extremes of intensity (brightness and colour) and unnecessary intensity variations.

Special gimmicks at sign-on or between screens may be attractive to first-time users of an application, but if they are time-consuming they can become irritating to someone who uses the package frequently. The main aim of having a computer is to speed up the work of the user – let your programs give the maximum assistance with the minimum of interference.

Having a standard design philosophy ensures that there is no major variation in the method of data entry from screen to screen within the application. The user quickly learns the conventions of the package and does not have to adjust to each new screen in a different way.

The messages the program offers the user are of many types:

- error reports produced by validation routines, and by procedures that write to files
- help messages explaining difficult or unusual procedures
- prompts (requests) for data entry
- system messages explaining long delays or system problems.

One standard practice is to allot special areas on the screen to different message types. This allows the user to adjust to each new screen more easily, and also gives the programmer the freedom to display and erase messages of one type without affecting any of the others.

The same errors and special conditions can come up at many different points within a program – so it is a good idea to have a consistent approach when handling these. It is therefore better to have modules dedicated to error and special conditions, and to re-use these at different points, as required.

Today, most programs that accept data onto backing storage work interactively via a screen. The usefulness of these programs depends on the programmer's ability to design screens which:

- are easy to read and fill out as forms
- allow free cursor movement for easy correction and verification of the input data
- give messages that are easy to interpret.

All data entry programs must also have routines that validate the data input. As one of the safeguards against incorrect entries, it is necessary to accumulate and display data-entry statistics giving the number of records entered and the errors found – then the data entry operator can check these incorrect records against the original source. Control totals (a sort of data entry check) should also be shown to ensure all data has been entered.

A good practice in a data entry program is to present some kind of key to the latest value entered – an operator often has to continue to work through interruptions which cause the last entry made to be forgotten.

One of the most important facilities required by the user is the ability to abort an entry at any point. Thus do not make it necessary to fill out an entire form if one wishes to cancel the entry. This requires a certain flexibility in the control which terminates the entry of one screen of data.

Screen handling facilities vary greatly, depending on the machine and the compiler version used. The screen section and "on escape" facility of Microsoft COBOL provide a simple way to introduce the required flexibility. In other versions of COBOL each item on the screen must be independently accepted and then checked to determine whether an abort has been requested.

When the number of data items to be entered is large and the items have complex structures and inter-relationships, a particular entry may be divided into more than one record while writing to a file. If the entry is cancelled after one screenful has been accepted, it would be necessary to check the file to ensure that there are no half entries. This problem can be overcome by keeping a count of records written and deleting all related records when required. Whenever possible it is better practice to store all the data corresponding to one entry until the entry is complete – and only then to write all the related records. In some software systems the user must keep track of related records and add or erase them when necessary.

Data entry programs allow the user to enter new data or to edit (amend) existing data. A screen for editing previous data looks like a data entry screen, but, instead of having blank areas to be filled in, shows the existing record so the user can decide whether to make any changes. A good program will allow you to move to any data field easily, either retaining or amending the intermediate data items as you wish.

Any screen-oriented program must ask users what they want done. This normally involves listing a number of options with a prompt saying how to choose. The choice leads to the next appropriate screen. This gives us a hierarchy ("tree") of screens through which the user can enter or leave any option.

As in all applications you must allow the user to quit or abort a certain level and return to an earlier one (or quit the program altogether) whenever desired. Thus if a wrong key entry is made, the situation can immediately be recovered by cancelling the selection at the next level. In short, any menu (options list) should always contain "escape" as one of the choices. Similarly, when a particular action has been concluded, it is better to present the next higher level menu again and allow the user to decide the next move, rather than asking "Do you wish to continue?" over and over again.

Page formatting and printing

The next step is the production of output. Printing on screens provides one option, but printed reports are more permanent. The stationery used can be continuous or consist of single sheets. Sometimes the system design will demand preprinted forms (documents containing fixed spaces which will be filled in with printed data from the computer).

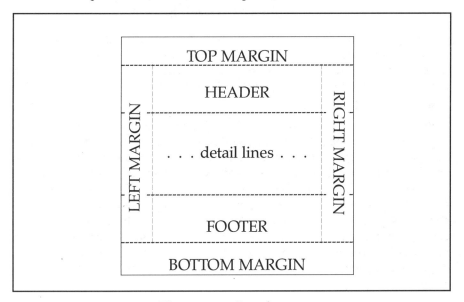

Figure 4.11   Page layout

The length of the paper and the number of characters to appear on each line are usually fixed by the systems analyst; the number of lines is a maximum of six per inch: for example, 11 inch paper will allow up to 66 lines on each page. Normally there are unused areas of between three and ten lines at the top of the page, and between five and ten lines at the bottom – the top and bottom margins. The rest of the page forms the print area. This is further divided into a heading area, a place for the body of the report, and a footing area. The header usually comprises a main heading line, one or more blank lines, then a line of column headings. Between these and the detail lines, there is usually a line of dashes, or other special characters, as shown in Figure 4.11.

To centre a heading on a line, count the number of characters on the heading, including spaces between words. Subtract this number from the number of available print positions on each line (eg, 80) to get the total number of blank spaces around the heading. Dividing this number by 2 gives the number of spaces that should be inserted in front of the heading.

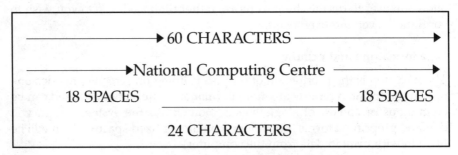

Figure 4.12 Headings

For example, assume that there are 60 characters per line, and the heading is National Computing Centre. Including spaces that is 24 characters in the heading, which leaves 60 − 24 = 36 spaces to be divided: 18 to the left, and 18 to the right of the heading as shown in Figure 4.12.

The detail lines which contain all the actual data will be printed until either the page or the data comes to an end. If the columns are all the same width, then to produce evenly spaced columns, divide the width of the paper by the number of columns required. This gives the number of characters per column including spaces. If the columns are different widths, then you can find the number of spaces between them as follows: add all the column widths to get the number of print positions needed, then subtract this from the number of available characters on the line. Remember to use the size of the column heading, if this is bigger than the size of the data, in the calculation. To calculate the number of spaces per column from this value, divide it by the number of columns + 1. This also provides an equal number of spaces for the left and right hand margins.

Take for example this case: there are three columns, the first 15 characters wide, the second 10, and the third 12. In total, we need 37 print positions. From a 60 print position line this leaves 60 − 37 = 23 spaces, to be distributed between 3 + 1 areas. Obviously, this doesn't produce a set of equal widths, but it may be that more space is needed for the left hand margin, so that the prints can have holes punched for filing. The page could be laid out as in Figure 4.13.

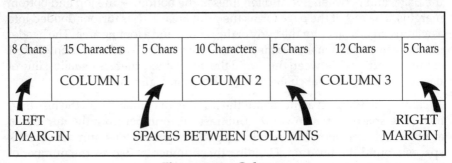

Figure 4.13 Columns

Normally software aligns the contents of each column differently according to whether they are characters or numbers. Characters are left aligned, that is with the first letters in the column in line under each other; whole numbers are right aligned (the last digits below each other); real numbers (with a decimal part) have the decimal points aligned. Figure 4.14 shows what I mean.

CHARACTERS	WHOLE NUMBERS	DECIMAL NUMBERS
MERNAGH	1 0 4	3 3 . 6
HUGHES	2 0 3 4	1 0 2 . 3 9
RICHARDS	6 5	3 . 8
WEST	2	1 0 6 . 8 9 3
BLACKLOCK	1 0 9 6 5	6 . 2
SIMPSON	2 3	1 0 9 . 1

Figure 4.14   Alignment

Headings for columns can appear in various ways. If the heading is longer than the data items, then we can centre those under the heading; on the other hand, if the data item is bigger, then the heading can be centred within the column. In fact, people often right align the headings for non-numeric data, and left align those for numeric data. This way both very large and very small data strings will be placed correctly in relation to the heading; Figure 4.15 should make this clearer.

ITEM	QTY	RATE
BULB	9 3	5 . 0 0
MACHINE SCREWS	5 8 , 7 4 4	0 . 1 0
SWITCH	1 9 9	0 . 7 5

Figure 4.15   Column headings

Most reports use the key field to determine the order in which the data prints out. The key field can vary depending on the use to which the report is being put; for example, student information (such as names, subjects and grades), might be sorted into alphabetic order to produce a list of students, or into subject order to determine the students who had enrolled for a particular subject. The convention for printing out this information is that the leftmost column should contain the key field – ie student name for the first list, and subject name for the second list. This makes it easier for the user to interpret the information.

If for any reason this arrangement is not possible, then insert an extra line in the report heading to tell the order in which the lines have been printed. Our last example was printed out in alphabetic order of item; if the key were changed to print in descending order of rates, the result would be Figure 4.16. Or we could keep the table as before and add "(in order of rateable value)" to the heading.

RATE	ITEM	QTY
5.00	BULB	93
0.75	SWITCH	199
0.10	MACHINE SCREWS	58,744

Figure 4.16   Ordering

Usually column totals appear at the end of the report. However, if the report end coincides with the end of a page, then these totals would have to be printed on their own at the top of the next page. It is not good to separate the last data item from the rest, so, to ensure this never happens, there is a special area called a footer on each page. The footer usually consists of the number of lines needed to print the total, but is left blank on every page except the last page of the report. Sometimes the footer is also used for sub-totals, page numbers or marks indicating that a continuation sheet follows.

Now we come to the actual printing. A printing algorithm should correspond to the three physical parts of a report. The printing of the detail lines forms the main loop, whilst the printing of the main heading and the final footers comprise the initialisation and termination sections. The flow of the main loop is broken for the preparation and ending of each page. These points are called control breaks. The code which produces the headings, footings and monitors the page breaks should be contained in independent modules. These can then be called from different program areas as required.

In Figure 4.17 is some pseudocode which represents an example of the kind of design that could be used.

```
                        Top-level design
            initialise;
            obtain data;
            if not end-of-data
               then print headings;
            endif;
            while not end-of-data
               do
                  set up line;
                  if linecount = footing-line
                     then print page-footings;
                     skip page;
                     print headings;
                     initialise linecount;
                  endif;
                  print line;
                  increment linecount;
                  obtain next data;
               endo;
            print end of report footings;
            terminate;
```

Figure 4.17   Top level design

The initialisation phase would include zeroising the line count used to recognise when the end of page condition is met. The obtain-data module would depend on the application (eg, read a file or a keyboard). The very first page heading appears only after making certain that there is some data to print. Before each line appears the program checks the amount of space left on the page, and, if it finds an end-of-page condition, carries out the correct action. Thus each print-line will find the paper ready for it.

Other forms of this algorithm follow setting up flags (special logical variables to mark certain events) to indicate conditions like end-of-page, or coding the whole process as a set of nested loops.

There is often a need to produce the print in a more complex structure than simple page breaks with an end of report total: for instance, we may need a sub-total when the value of a particular field changes. For processing the control break appropriate to this situation, the key of the first record is stored in a temporary variable at the beginning of the process and each new key is checked against its value. If it has changed, the page ending is processed, and the current key replaces the stored one. These modifications are required by the previous design; Figure 4.18. The key value is checked before the end-of-page condition, so that the page is not skipped before the key change is pressed.

```
        current-key ← key of first-record;
        while not end-of-data
          do
            set up line;
            if key <> current-key
              process key-change;
            endif;
            if end-of-page
              process page-ending;
            endif;
            print line;
            increment line-count;
            obtain next data;
          endo;

      Key-change;
      print end-key-footings;
      skip lines / page as required;
      current key ← key;
      print headings;
      update linecount;
```

Figure 4.18   Control breaks

If a sub-total were to be printed as part of the change in key routine, the control break would need at least the approach of Figure 4.19.

```
      prepare and print sub-total line;

      reset sub-total field;

      reset control field (store new key);

      set up page/spacing/headings for next sub-field;
```

Figure 4.19   Pseudocode for sub-total control break

4.6   CHECKING THE DESIGN

Once we have designed the logic of a program, it must be checked for correctness. This must be done before coding begins – mistakes become harder and more costly to correct the longer they remain in existence. If you have followed the systematic approach described in the foregoing chapters, you will have done much of the essential checking already. There is, however, one significant point to remember, and that is that the checking has probably been done by the author of the design, who will almost certainly fail to spot all the possible potential errors. Programmers should not be worried by this point. It is perfectly natural that, since the programmer presumably intends the program to be correct, it will always look good. Rather than waste too much time admiring your own work, it would be far more productive to allow someone else to check it over. Whilst this is going on you can, of course, check the work of another member of the team.

This "peer testing" can be a very revealing exercise – but there is a danger that colleagues may form a mutual admiration society: failing to be too critical of each other's work for fear of recriminations. One possible answer to this is to adopt a "worst enemy" approach, in which a programmer's work is checked by a non-colleague, who will try harder to discover mistakes. Such an approach will succeed only if we see the programming project as a team effort, rather than a set of individual contributions.

Various worthy, popular and distinct approaches to program design checking exist; they are in no way mutually exclusive. This is illustrated in Figure 4.20.

Figure 4.20   Checking methods

Dry running

This technique involves working through a piece of design code from your desk: the checker (often the programmer) pretends to be the computer carrying out the program. Take care to make a careful note (on paper) of the effect of each instruction in the program. This is particularly important when checking a loop, when there is a temptation to miss out a few steps because "you know what it does". The purpose of a dry run is to see what the code actually does, not what it is supposed to do! (The place to look for the latter information is, of course, the design specification.) Once an often-used sub-process has been thoroughly checked, it may of course be accepted as correct until proved otherwise.

It is seldom a good idea to attempt to dry run a large amount of design code at once. If the systematic approach is followed, a dry run may be carried out at any level of refinement. If possible, an entire process should be checked at a high level before refinement goes too far.

To prepare for a dry run, take a large piece of paper (old listings are useful here) and mark it out with a column for each variable used in the code to be checked. Write in each column the appropriate initial value, if any, for the variable. The required values can be obtained either from the data dictionary or from knowledge of previous program conditions.

Now proceed to work through the design code, one instruction at a time, simulating its effect. Note in the appropriate places on your paper the new values of variables as they change. If there are conditional expressions involved in your code, keep track of their values too. Provided that you are careful to follow the code, and can avoid trying to anticipate what is going to happen, you should be reproducing the action of your program when run by the computer. If your dry run fails to reach a proper end, you have a written record, or trace, of the action of your design from which you can correct it.

You will soon discover that such a technique can be very time-consuming: and it may not yield the desired effect if always carried out by the programmer responsible for the design.

The walk-through

This second technique has been described formally by several authors. The approach adopted here is less formal than most, but may be adjusted to suit local requirements.

The basic idea is for the author of a design to expose it to a collection of his colleagues for 'group criticism'. In its most formal form, an invitation is sent to a number of interested persons, NOT INCLUDING MANAGEMENT PERSONNEL, together with copies of all relevant documents. At the meeting one of the participants will act as a secretary and note everything that is said. The author of the design describes what has been done and why. Other participants raise queries or suggest possible pit-falls. It is important that, at this stage, no attempt is made to SOLVE the difficulties, only to recognise them. At the end of the meeting, which should not last more than 45 minutes, the secretary hands the notes to the designer, who takes them away and tries to find solutions to all of the noted problems. This may involve redesigning part of the code, possibly with the assistance of other members of the team. The design author must document in some way, perhaps by annotating the record of the meeting, that all of the problems exposed have been solved.

Such an approach can be very valuable indeed, but will take some getting used to. Programmers are naturally reticent to expose their work, fearing ridicule. They must be encouraged by the thought that, eventually, all members of the team will be similarly exposed. Ideally, the first to do it should be a team-leader, so that other, perhaps less experienced, members of the team do not feel exposed.

There are many advantages to be gained from this approach to design checking. Some of them are:

- early exposure of problems
- interaction between team members
- education of team members
- constant awareness of progress
- consistency of design approach.

Catalytic checking

This is a much less formal approach to design checking: the designer tries to describe in detail to a single colleague exactly how the program works. The colleague appears in a purely passive role, occasionally asking "why?" or "how?". So designers can describe their work to such poor listeners, they must examine every part of the design very carefully, and be able to justify every step.

A good colleague will help a great deal, without actually assuming anything about the author's work; remember to say "thank you for listening", and be prepared to do the same in exchange another time.

Independent inspection

This approach involves the designer handing work to a colleague to go through alone. The colleague may walk through or dry run the design, or simply study it: the point is that a separate view may bring to light hitherto unrecognised problems. This technique is often adopted by a senior programmer, who will "inspect" a junior's work before discussing it.

Egoless programming

You will have noted that all these design checking techniques involve exposure of your work to other people. It is most important that individual team members are encouraged to do this right from the start. Unfortunately, many people find this difficult to accept, but it is worth persevering with. Much has been written about "egoless" programming, meaning "this is not my program but our program", and this approach may encourage closer inspection of work by all concerned. However, programmers must take a pride in their work and be prepared to say "I did that", rather than whispering "I'm afraid it is mine."

The acceptance of the group criticism approach to program design checking can be encouraged by ensuring that management personnel are excluded from walk throughs, and that everyone understands that the programmer's career prospects must not in any way be affected by how many mistakes are discovered in the work at such sessions. If the right approach to design is adopted, then this early discovery of errors will turn out to be a lot cheaper in the long run.

NOW TRY THESE . . .

Exercise One

A program for an on-line bulletin board accepts a code from each customer after displaying an introductory message. Using pseudocode, design the validation routine for the customer code.

NOTE: An external routine BILLING exists elsewhere which measures the time that the customer uses the bulletin board and calculates the appropriate cost; this should be called if the validation checks are completely satisfactory.

Exercise Two

Assuming the details supplied in Chapter 3 Exercise 1 (except for the flowchart) were given to you as a specification, compile a list of points which would need further clarification or which are not explained fully.

5   Coding

OBJECTIVES

When you have worked through this chapter, you should be able to:
- explain the necessity for coding standards
- explain the need for readable code, and describe several ways to obtain it
- apply the concept of modules (procedures) to the production of maintainable code
- state the principles of coding in a high level program language from an outline algorithm
- apply these principles in practice
- briefly describe the normal steps between coding and running the program
- state how compiled and interpreted programs differ at each step, including as regards diagostics.

INTRODUCTION

After you've specified and designed the program – and checked the design with care – coding is the next stage.

In this chapter, we explore a number of general points and techniques. However, we'll also see how to convert major algorithm structures into code in COBOL, FORTRAN and minimal (ie, old) Basic.

Those general points are most important – they apply whatever program language you work with (at least if the language has adequate power and range of features). All the same, it will also help you get some feel for the three languages we've chosen to work with here.

5.1 CODING STANDARDS

There are two main functions performed by programming: the creation of programs, and the maintenance of existing programs. The former involves the initial writing of code and its subsequent checking and amendment so that it performs its required functions; and the latter: the changing and adding of features as required.

Without control of any kind a programmer producers code which reflects his interest in the job, expertise, and to some extent personality. At the earliest stages of his career the inexperienced programmer uses the simplest techniques to produce the required solution, which may not always be the most efficient. As experience grows the programmer develops a style. Sometimes this is arbitrary – using the names of friends for data-names is one almost everyone will recognise – but more often it is a kind of shorthand used to try to speed up the production of code (which is always behind schedule). Once the principle of say nested IF statements is understood, then it becomes easy to write and thus provide a quick solution to a problem. The justification for this might be considered acceptable if the originator of the code was always available to make changes to his programs, and he could always remember what he was trying to do and how he did it. Unfortunately this is seldom the case. Often the programmer moves on, either to new programs or applications, and is not available to answer queries. Even if he remains working on the same program, when it examining the code months, or even weeks, later, the programmer is unlikely to be able to recall what he did, how he did it and why. It is therefore relatively safe to assume that maintenance will be done by someone who has either never seen the code before or has little recall of it, and since the majority of the time which will be used changing the program will be taken up in trying to understand it and deciding what to change, it makes sense to reduce this as much as possible. By laying down rules to be followed, standards provide a way of ensuring that consistent quality is maintained throughout all areas of programming from design methods to coding style. Although coding has been emphasised here, the principles apply equally to program design, construction, and testing. It is essential that the tasks which make up program production are undertaken in a disciplined way, otherwise it is not possible to achieve quality, undertake accurate planning, measure results realistically, or even control the activities involved. Standards can provide a framework to ensure that a disciplined approach is cultivated from the earliest stages of a programmer's, designer's or analyst's development which will remain for as long as it is encouraged to do so. Standards help inexperienced programmers to become effective more quickly, and by making programs easier to comprehend, amend, and check, they help experienced programmers to become more productive. Standards aid communication between people working on the same project and increase the interchangeability of people with different aptitudes, abilities, and experience, within and between different projects.

5.2 A READABLE PROGRAM

People often say that the readability of a program is much more important than the intricacies of its code. If you have followed the systematic approach to program design discussed earlier, the logic of your program will be obvious and meaningful. Take care to preserve this readability when coding, when producing the actual program instructions.

Here is a list of the relevant aspects of the coding stage:

1   If the program language imposes very strict limits, include a translation table, relating data names to labels. You will need this only when using some older versions of Basic or FORTRAN: most other languages allow plenty of freedom in naming variables. Remember that the use of a maximum-size character name in COBOL in now way effects the run time efficiency of your program, but may make it much more readable.

Meaningful names make program code easier to read. Look at this example:

ADD A TO B GIVING C

A, B and C could be anything, but if they are replaced with names like:
        INTEREST
        CURRENT-BALANCE
        OUTSTANDING-AMOUNT
things become clearer:

ADD INTEREST TO CURRENT-BALANCE GIVING OUTSTANDING-AMOUNT

The more complex the program, the more important meaningful names become, not only for the variables but also for the program name, the paragraph names, the subroutine names and the file names.

RULES FOR DATA NAMES
i   Use names that describe the purpose of the code or variable, eg; CALCU-LATE-DISCOUNT, or GROSS-PAY.
    ii   Don't make up aliases.
    iii Don't use names that are similar, change at least two letters.
    iv   Keep spellings as normal as possible, eg: EMPLOYER-NAME rather than EMPLOYA-NAM.. if the language rules don't allow this, then use abbreviations consistently, eg: FIRST-NAME to FRST-NM.
    v   Use the same prefix for all the variables in one record or the local variables in a subroutine.
    vi   Before deciding on names, cross-reference to any existing data dictionary definitions and ensure agreement from the data administrator for the ones used.

2   Include a complimentary (plenty of remarks or comments). All program languages let you use comments in a source program. Make adequate use of these facilities.

Comments help us to understand the purpose of each module and then to remember it. At the module level the comments should contain a description of:

 – The module function;

 – Date of last revision;

 – Inputs and outputs;

 – Variables used.

For example:

TEST-AGE-GROUP.

THIS MODULE CHECKS THE AGE OF EACH INDIVIDUAL AND ALLO-CATES AN APPROPRIATE AGE GROUP CODE

VARIABLES USED IN THIS MODULE
    MANS-DOB
    WOMANS-DOB
    AGE-GROUP-TABLE
    AGE-GROUP

MODULE LAST REVISED 02/01/93

Whilst it is a good thing to include comments for some lower-level features such as tables, it is not necessary to add them to each line of code. They should only be used for explaining complicated algorithms, or hightlighting error-prone sections of the program. Remember to always include a blank line before and after any comments.

It is well worth taking trouble with comments – remember that anyone reading your program will not necessarily understand why you wrote it that way unless you tell them. (Also, six months after the event, you will probably have forgotten why yourself!)

3   Lay out the code clearly. Your code will be much easier to follow if you lay it out neatly across the page. Make proper use of indentation to reflect the logic structure of the code (unless your language does not allow this), and do not try to cram too much code on one line. It is a good idea to place only one instruction on each line – this will make later changes much simpler. Also, make sensible use of blank lines and new pages to keep the code readable, and limit components to a manageable size.

4   Avoid "tricks" – always make sure you write straightforward code which people can readily understand. The novelty of a "clever dodge" will soon wear off, especially if the person who wrote it left two years ago and YOU have to unravel it! Remember that it is seldom worth striving to save a few machine instructions by using trick coding – the micro-seconds gained will be much less than the time spent in effort.

5.3 A MAINTAINABLE PROGRAM

Maintaining is keeping a program up-to-date after it has been written and put into use. This is important work for programmers because it is estimated that up to 80% of all the effort expended on a program throughout its life can be attributed to its maintenance. Maintenance changes are generally the result of one of the following:

- errors being found in the way that the program *actually* works, compared to *how* it should work;

- statutory changes that affect the company and its computer system, eg: government policy;

- internal changes in the business, either in the structure of the organisation or in the way that it carries out business, eg: mergers and the introduction of other computer systems.

These changes are likely to affect the code in existing programs, so we will look at that aspect in detail; first however let's take a step away from the code and look at the program structure. A logical program structure can help in making the code traceable (easy to follow) so that what needs to be changed can be found easily.

5.3.1 Modularisation

The aim in splitting up a program is to make it easier to understand, but by creating the independent chunks of code that we will call modules we also reduce the effort needed later when changes to the program are required. This is because:

- if the function that is performed by a module changes, only the code in that module needs to be changed and the rest of the program stays the same;

- if a new feature is added to the program then a new module is added, and the rest of the program is unaffected;

- making modules independent makes designing tests easier;

- having independent modules makes finding errors easier.

Rules for modules
1   Each module should contain only one program function.
2   The maximum size for each module should be 100 instructions.
3   There should only be one entry point and one exit point in each module.

5.3.2 Structured programs

It is all very well breaking up a program into modules, but if there is no sequence or order in their structure then half the benefit is lost. The properties of well-structured programs are as follows:

- the program modules are arranged in a hierarchy which mirrors the way that they work logically;

- when the programs begins to run the modules are executed in turn. Each module has only one entry and one exit point and when finished it passes control back to the module that called it.

This means that the program structure looks like that shown in Figure 5.1.

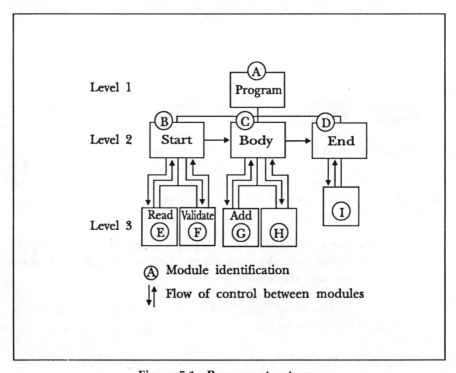

Figure 5.1   Program structure

5.4 CODING TECHNIQUES

Any good programmer will know how to use the particular program language to express the operations contained in the program design. It is nevertheless worthwhile for an installation, or at least a project team, to adopt some local standard techniques for handling fundamental constructs. The adoption of such standards will enable systematic translation of a program design into code and, as I pointed out earlier, a systematic approach is more likely to be successful.

When the ELSE part of a conditional is missing, care must be taken with the coding....

COBOL:

IF GROSS-PAY < BAND-1

PERFORM LOWER-BAND.

FORTRAN:

IF (GPAY .LT. BAND1) CALL LBAND

(b)   (the multi selection)

IF condition-1

THEN sequence-1;

ELSE IF condition-2

THEN sequence-2;

ELSE sequence-3;

ENDIF;

This is an example of a "nested IF" construct with null alternatives. Again, it can be coded in COBOL directly.

IF KODE = 1
PERFORM ADDITION
ELSE IF KODE = 2
PERFORM DELETION
ELSE IF KODE = 3
PERFORM CHANGE-ADDRESS
ELSE IF KODE = 4
PERFORM CHANGE-NAME
ELSE IF KODE = 5
PERFORM CHANGE-CREDIT
ELSE PERFORM ERROR-CODE.
PERFORM NEXT-P.

This is a fairly clean nested IF, and it is clear what logic is involved. It could have been coded as a GO TO...DEPENDING ON, as follows, this being the equivalent of the CASE construct in early versions of COBOL.

Below are shown suggested standards, included as examples only – each installation or team will produce their own.

1   Program structure – in COBOL a component of the program design will probably appear as a SECTION. A decision must be made about the order of such sections in the program.

2   Conditional commands – when refining from the universal program, two forms of conditional (selective) construct may be used:

(a)   **IF condition**

        THEN command-sequence;

        ELSE command-sequence;

    ENDIF;

When coding this in COBOL, it may be written more or less as it stands, the final ENDIF becoming a full stop. By using the same layout convention, a more readable result is achieved:

    IF GROSS-PAY < BAND-1

        PERFORM LOWER-BAND

    ELSE   PERFORM UPPER-BAND

When coding in FORTRAN, it is not easy to avoid the use of a GOTO. Perhaps, best code the above example as:

    IF (GPAY .LT. BAND1) GOTO 1001

        CALL UBAND

        GOTO 1002

  1001   CALL LBAND

  1002   CONTINUE

By using this universal translation structure, more complicated examples can be handled without extra difficulty. Indeed, the above FORTRAN "expansion" can be made automatically by a suitable pre-processor.

```
GO TO P-ADDITION
        P-DELETION
        P-CHANGE-ADDRESS
        P-CHANGE-NAME
        P-CHANGE-CREDIT
        DEPENDING ON KODE.
        PERFORM ERROR-CODE.
        GO TO GO-COLLECT.

        P-ADDITION.
          PERFORM ADDITION.

          GO TO GO-COLLECT.
        P-DELETION.
          PERFORM DELETION
          GO TO GO-COLLECT.
        P-CHANGE-ADDRESS.
          PERFORM CHANGE-ADDRESS
          GO TO GO-COLLECT.
        P-CHANGE-NAME.
          PERFORM CHANGE-NAME
          GO TO GO-COLLECT.
        P-CHANGE-CREDIT.
          PERFORM CHANGE-CREDIT
          GO TO GO-COLLECT.
        GO-COLLECT.
          PERFORM NEXT-P.
```

Notice how the last alternative executes a GO TO to reach GO-COLLECT in order to simplify the later addition of further options. It should be borne in mind that structured programs should never need to contain a GO TO command. However, before structured commands like WHILE . . . DO were included in languages they were very common. They should not be used where structured constructs are available as they are the chief cause of spaghetti code (see earlier).

FORTRAN offers a computed GOTO as with:

```
        IF (KODE .LT. 1 .OR. KODE .GT. 5) GOTO 6000
        GOTO (1000, 2000, 3000, 4000, 5000), KODE
1000 CALL ADDSUB
        GOTO 7000
2000 CALL DELSUB
        GOTO 7000
3000 CALL CADSUB
        GOTO 7000
4000 CALL CNMSUB
        GOTO 7000
5000 CALL CCRSUB
        GOTO 7000
6000 CALL ERRSUB
        GOTO 7000
7000 CALL PNEXT
```

A third alternative method of coding a multiway selection is to use simple conditions:

```
        IF KODE = 1
          PERFORM ADDITION.
        IF KODE = 2
          PERFORM DELETION.
        IF KODE = 3
          PERFORM CHANGE-ADDRESS.
        IF KODE = 4
          PERFORM CHANGE-NAME.
        IF KODE = 5
          PERFORM CHANGE-CREDIT.
        IF KODE < 1
          PERFORM ERROR-CODE.
        IF KODE > 5
          PERFORM ERROR-CODE.
        PERFORM NEXT-P.
```

In this case the coding is simpler, but there are two minor disadvantages. First, it is not immediately obvious that only one of these seven conditions can be true: therefore program clarity suffers. Second, all seven conditions will be tested before PERFORM NEXT-P is executed, even if the first is true: making the other six unnecessary. A further disadvantage of this code is that if the acceptable values of KODE are changed or extended, the subsequent changes to the code are more complex than in the earlier example.

Another point here concerns the ordering of conditions in a multi selection. Obviously some execution time may be saved by placing the test for the most often occurring condition first, but take care not to obscure the logic in this way.

(Note: in many languages, such as Pascal and Ada, the multi selection has its own special syntax: learn and exploit it.)

3   Loop control: in Chapter 1 we looked at three forms of this.

(a) **WHILE condition**
            DO command-sequence;
            ENDDO;

This is the safest form of loop control when the number of repetitions required is not known in advance. It may be coded in COBOL74, using PERFORM...UNTIL, as in the following example.

            WHILE sum $<$ = maxsum
            DO accumulate-next-term;
            ENDO;

would appear as:

            PERFORM ACCUMULATE-NEXT-TERM
            UNTIL SUM $>$ MAX-SUM.

Note that the condition used in the WHILE must be inverted for use in the UNTIL clause. Observe also that the condition in the UNTIL clause is evaluated BEFORE the PERFORM section is executed for the first time.

In COBOL85, using the WITH TEST BEFORE option also allows the condition to be tested before the code is executed, as in:

            PERFORM ACCUMULATE-NEXT-TERM
            WITH TEST BEFORE
            UNTIL SUM $>$ MAX-SUM.

When using languages such as old FORTRAN or Basic, which do not have many sensible control constructs available, the while loop must be encoded using conditional and unconditional GOTO statements. Let us first translate the while loop using our universal language.

> **WHILE condition**
> **DO command-sequence;**
> **ENDO;**

becomes

> **label 1: IF NOT condition THEN GOTO label 2;**
> **command-sequence;**
> **GOTO label 1;**
> **label 2: {next command sequence}**

This version may easily be expressed in FORTRAN or Basic (using our earlier example) as:

> **1000   IF (SUM .GT. MAXSUM) GO TO 2000**
> **CALL ANXTRM (SUM)**
> **GO TO 1000**
> **2000   CONTINUE**

or

> **100   IF s > m THEN GOTO 130**
> **110   GOSUB 1000**
> **120   GOTO 100**
> **130   REM NEXT COMMAND**

(b)   Next is the REPEAT loop:

> **REPEAT**
> **command-sequence;**
> **UNTIL condition;**

Take care when coding this construct using COBOL 74, since our REPEAT...UNTIL loop requires the controlled command sequence to be executed once before the condition is evaluated. Therefore the sequence

> **REPEAT**
> **accumulate-next-term;**
> **UNTIL sum > maxsum;**

must be coded in COBOL as:

PERFORM ACCUMULATE-NEXT-TERM.

PERFORM ACCUMULATE-NEXT-TERM

UNTIL SUM > MAX-SUM.

(because the UNTIL is evaluated before the PERFORM to which it applies is executed).

This has been simplified in COBOL85 by the WITH TEST AFTER option. It is now possible to code the previous example as:

PERFORM ACCUMULATE-NEXT-TERM

WITH TEST AFTER

UNTIL SUM > MAX-SUM.

(c)   The FOR... loop is for use when the programmer knows how many times the program needs to run through the loop's command sequence.

FOR kount FROM 1 TO 100

DO print-statement;

ENDO;

This may be coded in COBOL as:

PERFORM PRINT-STATEMENT

VARYING KOUNT FROM 1 BY 1

UNTIL KOUNT > 100.

assuming that PRINT-STATEMENT is a remote SECTION in the program. There is, by the way, a school of thought which favours writing UNTIL KOUNT = 100, and placing the code for PRINT-STATEMENT immediately following the PERFORM...UNTIL. This is bad practice, for a number of reasons: first, the program is less readable because the controlled actions and control statements are mixed; second, it makes maintenance more open to error.

The FORTRAN and Basic versions of this form of loop are very straight forward; however, realise that, in both cases, the uncontrolled command sequence will always be executed at least once. Since the universal language does not assume this, guard the appropriate statements with a conditional GOTO if the end-point of the control range is a variable. So, best code

FOR i FROM 1 to N

DO

print-value;

ENDO;

as

```
        IF (N .LT. 1) GO TO 2000
        DO 1000 I=1,N
            CALL PRTVAL
1000 CONTINUE
2000 CONTINUE
```

or

```
100 IF n < 1 THEN GOTO 140
110 FOR i = 1 TO n
120 GOSUB 1000
130 NEXT i
140 next command
```

Note that a CONTINUE statement as the terminal statement of a DO-loop in FORTRAN will both enhance readability and avoid problems with incorrect nesting or termination.

5.5 SOME GENERAL POINTS

The following comments apply in any programming project. Proper attention to them can save a lot of time, otherwise spent debugging bad code.

1 Conditionals involving real numbers

Since a computer can handle real (ie fractional) numbers only approximately within a computer, never test two such numbers for equality. Instead, test to see if their values differ by an amount less than some agreed limit. Such a precaution will always be necessary in FORTRAN, Basic, Pascal, and Algol, and may also be necessary if you use COMPUTATIONAL values in COBOL. Thus, instead of

```
IF (A .EQ. B) GO TO 100
```

use

```
IF (ABS (A−B) .LT. TOL) GO TO 100
```

Here TOL contains the agreed tolerance value. In some circumstances this procedure may be simplified, by making a test for $<$, for example, at the end of a loop including a summation. Thus, do not code:

```
100 SUM = SUM + X
    IF (SUM .NE. Y) GO TO 100
```

but instead code:

```
100 SUM = SUM + X
    IF (SUM .LT. Y) GO TO 100
```

2 Compound conditions

Most program languages allow you to build conditional expressions from several simple conditions linked with operators such as AND and OR. Take care with these. Many programmers, especially beginners, experience some difficulty here, especially when using the operator NOT. Perhaps never use both AND and NOT (or OR and NOT) in the same expression.

Also take care to realise that, though the value of a conditional expression may be found without evaluating all of its terms, very few program language systems exploit this. Thus, when programming a table-look-up, one often writes a condition such as

$$(i > tabsize) \text{ OR } (key = table[i])$$

to determine loop termination. Unfortunately, a program which uses such a condition directly will probably fail in the case when the sought item is not in the table. This is because, though the fact that $(i > tabsize)$ is true is enough to make the whole expression true, most systems will in any case try to evaluate $(key = table[i])$: and get a "subscript out of range" message. Some program languages provide special syntax to cater for this situation (like the OR ELSE of Ada), but the best solution is to avoid it.

3 Data value initialisation

By far the safest approach is to incorporate explicit assignments to move initial values into data items. Though program languages allow such values to be built in at compile time, a maintenance programmer may fail to observe the significance of initial values when studying the procedure division unless there are such assignments.

4 Coding data

Most program languages do not offer much choice for how to represent data items. The most notable exceptions are COBOL and Pascal/Ada. In COBOL it is recommended that allocations used for arithmetic should be declared in WORKING-STORAGE with USAGE COMPUTATIONAL. This will make the program more run-time efficient with no loss of clarity. COBOL programmers should also be aware of how data items are stored in their particular system, so they can reach sensible decisions about the use of SYNCHRONISED data. It is often possible to achieve considerable savings of space by re-ordering the items within a data structure declaration.

5 Separation of data and code

Most program languages enforce the physical separation of data and procedural code (the notable exception being assembly language). Care must be taken to reflect this separation when constructing programs; wider use of level 88 condition names in COBOL can help here. For example, if, instead of making the explicit test

IF KODE = 1

THEN PERFORM ADDITION

we were to use a level 88 condition name in the declaration of KODE:

02   KODE   PIC9.

88   ADDKODE   VALUE 1.

we could use

IF ADDKODE

THEN PERFORM ADDITION

This is more readable, and also has the advantage that, should the transaction code for an addition be changed from 1 to some other value, the only change to make is in the DATA declaration. This is helpful since the change is to the data and not to the program logic.

6 Guard code

When coding a multi selection, always include an explicit test for every possibility. For example, with the transaction codes of 1 to 5, which we used earlier, it would not be safe to assume that the value must be 5 if it were none of 1, 2, 3 or 4. Even if a previous process had already rejected invalid values, it is better to test explicitly for all five – this will make the program clearer and easier to maintain.

Also, should the previous process be modified to accept a new, valid, code 6, before the process has been modified, it is much better to treat the new code as an error, than to treat it as a "change-credit". This adds run-time security.

5.6 SOURCE FILES

If you have followed the procedures described so far, you will now have a version of the program containing data description and encoded in the required program language. The next stage in the development of the program is to produce an executable program ready for running on the computer.

Source file creation

When the coded program is ready for entering into the computer, it passes through a data conversion system; this automatically generates the ASCII or corresponding code for each letter. The result goes in a file called a source file, eventually input to the compiler.

Depending on the language used, the format can be fixed or you can be free to enter code anywhere on the line. Many of the earlier languages, for historical reasons, had restrictions in the use of character positions.

The present trend is for on-line entry through suitable terminal devices. However, there may be a data entry operator, in which case the program will have to be written out carefully, line by line, on special coding sheets with each character unambiguously formed and each character position clearly defined. Figure 5.2 shows coding sheets for FORTRAN and COBOL. Each line has 80 columns, for 80 character positions; some of the columns can be used only for certain types of data. Thus, FORTRAN uses character positions 1—5 for numbering those statements which require a label (generally for branching and iterative procedures); position 6 is to tell the compiler that the current line is a continuation of the previous line. Positions beyond 72 are used as a serial number for the line, and are ignored by the compiler. A comment line is indicated by a special character in column 1.

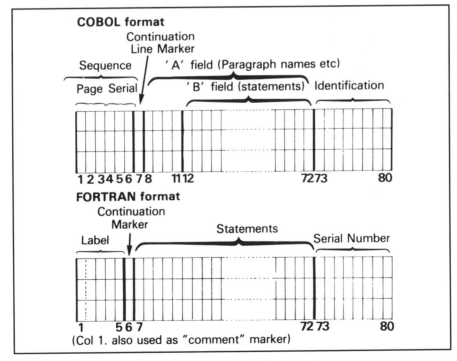

Figure 5.2   Examples of format sheets

Interactive entry can greatly speed up the development process and enhance the productivity of the programmer – but it can tempt you to take short-cuts and develop the code, or even the logic, on-line. Except in the most trivial cases, this results in bad programs. This does not mean that you should never code into the system directly – but it does mean that you should not try to write code into a terminal directly from the specification, designing and developing the code as you type it. It may be good for an author to type straight into a word processor – but programmers should not work that way. Design and checking are definitely "off-line" activities – and so, in all but the most trivial cases, is coding.

Only when the program has been designed, coded and entered into the system should you access the files for editing purposes. Ideally, under those conditions, you will have ready access to a terminal and so can develop the habit of preparing file edits off-line, only using the terminal to edit and for test-compilation.

However carefully the program has been written, it is always possible to create errors while entering it, especially when this is done by an operator. Sometimes the staff may verify (check) it by eye; otherwise special verification programs allow the same data to be re-entered so the computer can compare the two versions. Any discrepancies are signalled for action. A different operator during re-entry further improves accuracy.

For the creation of source files some sort of "line-editor" package is on offer from the operating software (EDLIN in DOS for example). A much more advanced version can be found in many commonly available word-processing packages. These packages accept data in character (or text) format and display it on a monitor without trying to interpret it in any way. The data can be edited by changing words or inserting and deleting characters. It is then stored on disk or tape in a file. Line editors work on one line at a time, while word processors usually use the full display screen as a "page" of data, allowing you to move to any word easily. Word processors also offer many more facilities, like "search and replace", that make editing data easier.

As an alternative, at some installations, the source code file is created by a professional keyboard operator keying the information onto tape, or, more probably, disk. Since this person is not likely to be a programmer as well, you must take great care when writing out the source text.

The compiler

After the source text has been created and checked, it can go to the compiler for a first attempt at translation. A compiler for a high level language will combine several operations, the most important of which are the analysis and translation of the source code.

The analysis phase begins by scanning the code to ensure that it contains only recognisable elements and that they have been used correctly: eg IF and loop constructs properly terminated; data usage consistent, etc. The compiler will produce (either as a printout, or as a file) a numbered listing of the source code, and a list of the syntax errors found.

Novice programmers are often disappointed that the compiler does not also report errors in their logic. No-one should fall into the trap of believing that even when the compilation is error-free, the program is inevitably correct, or even sensible. Agreed, there is a popular saying among programmers that "you can't expect a program to work first time". This is true for the kind of error that can be detected by the compiler: but a program that has been developed systematically from a well-thought out design should be free of logical errors. For syntax errors one should aim to get the program correct in not more than three attempts.

Lastly, while it is very tempting to reorganise the logic of a program during on-line testing, resist such a practice. Any such reorganisation should be carried out away from the terminal, preferably by referring back to the design documentation rather than just to the program listing. If, after a session at the terminal, you decide it would be better to return to your desk and reconsider the program design, obtain an up-to-date listing of the program. It is very frustrating to spend possibly hours reconsidering a program only to discover that the stored file is not the same as the listed version.

Compile-time errors

Often compile-time errors will produce messages (diagnostics) which indicate not only the site of the error but also its probable cause; however, the computer can detect only inconsistencies and give the nearest possible message for what it finds. These cannot be taken too literally – further investigation may be needed to pinpoint the actual cause. There will be occasions when no explicit cause is detectable, and others when one error masks others from detection. Sometimes the detection of one error by the compiler may cause other errors. COBOL compilers in particular are prone to these avalanche errors. Thus an error in a data definition often results in a string of errors, one for each occasion when the false label appears.

Unfortunately not all compiler diagnostic messages are useful. Actual examples include: "The impossible has happened" and "This error is caused by other messages"! In this case the only significance that you can attach to the message is that something is definitely wrong; unfortunately the message may sometimes state the wrong cause, or suggest no cause at all.

Source file maintenance

The most convenient way for a programmer to indicate necessary corrections and/or alterations to the source text of a program is to mark the compiler-generated listing in some way. Take care to avoid the practice of so heavily deleting errors that the original text is no longer readable.

Once the corrections have been marked on the listing, and a final check has been made as to their correctness, steps may be taken to alter the source file to reflect these changes. The exact method of this source file maintenance of course depends on the form in which the file is kept. When working with an operator you must write the corrected lines on a coding sheet, and perhaps give the editing commands as well.

Some operating systems and editing packages maintain earlier versions of files under a different version number so that you can go back to a previous version. However, this can result in unnecessary copies taking up valuable space – unless you keep track and remove unwanted files every so often. Similarly, in the case of compilations which have failed, remove old listings and object files. Large computer systems periodically reorganise their storage, re-copying all files and re-dating them; thus the date written on the file is not a reliable indicator of which file contains the latest version. If the system offers you no help at all, you must incorporate your own version code into the program. At worst a comment or remark which you automatically update every time you recompile, showing perhaps your initials and the date, can save a lot of time in attempting to debug from an out-of-date listing.

Linkage

One can compile sub-modules and procedures in the program independently and then link them to produce an executable file. High-level commands and functions often use library routines; the compiler puts in references to these, but does not actually put them into the code. Thus the compiler output is a series of disjointed program segments stored in the object file. Briefly, the linker consolidates one or more object files as specified, attends to compiler messages, and adds essential codes to produce a loadable version of the program. The program is now ready for execution by the computer.

Interpreting

In an interactive environment some languages may be interpreted rather than compiled. Instead of being just a translator (with error detection as a by-product), an interpreter provides an interface through which you can create and maintain, translate and execute a source program.

The interpreter provides a word processor, or at least a line editor, for entering and editing source files. Translation is done at run-time and the interpreter remains in control during execution. Each instruction is "interpreted": ie checked for identifiable elements and internal consistency, translated into object code, and executed. In case of any fatal error the program stops, and the interpreter awaits an instruction from the user.

Thus, in comparison with a compiler, there is no object code version of a program, and the execution must take place in the interpreter environment. As each instruction is checked and translated on each run, execution is much slower. Even syntax errors can appear only at run-time. Any portion or branch of the code which is unused during testing could still have errors which will be detected only the first time it is used.

Some programmers' workbenches contain a "checking" option for source code. Quick testing and amending of source files is possible with an interpreter of this type. Program modules or sections can be developed, tested independently, and combined. However, after the testing is over, any useful programs must be compiled and their object code (final) versions put into place in the system.

NOW TRY THESE...

Exercise One

a) Two program qualities are mentioned in the text: readability and maintainability. Try to think of some others.

b) Readability has been broken down in the text into four component parts called "quality characteristics". They can be represented like this diagram:

	Meaningful data names
Readability	Adequate comments
	Layout of code
	Avoidance of tricks

List four rules that will improve maintainability (see text for details) and then for the other program qualities you thought of.

6   Testing and de-bugging

OBJECTIVES

When you have worked through this chapter, you should be able to:

- explain the need for thorough testing once a program is coded
- name and outline the three levels of program correctness
- state, with examples, how unit, integration, and system testing differ
- describe the processes of test scheduling and planning
- explain the nature of test harnesses and dummy stubs
- list the five components of a test description
- describe the methods of choice of test data items
- describe methods of de-bugging.

INTRODUCTION

Once you've coded your program, you must apply a range of tests to ensure:

- it does what it should
- it does it well and efficiently
- it does so without error.

Careful program design and coding much reduce the number of mistakes of these kinds – but always some remain. (Note that studies show that the later people find an error in a program, the more costly it is to correct.)

In this chapter, we explore that final testing stage. It involves running the program again and again with as wide a range of input data as possible, and checking the results. However good that testing process, still some errors always remain in any significant program. These errors are the bugs that the users find and have to put up with.

6.1   WHAT IS TESTING?

Testing is part of the procedures that ensure the program corresponds with the original specification, and that it works in its intended environment. We have already come across some similar verification and validation techniques. Dry running the code helps to ensure its logical correctness, and inspections and walk throughs are to confirm that no errors follow the transition from stage to stage, eg specification to design.

The difference between these activities and testing is that they are "static", while testing is "dynamic". Dynamic in this situation means the process uses executable code, rather than listings or documents which describe the code. Testing should form a major part of any verification and validation activity on any software project. Static methods can be used to very good effect, and contribute significantly to the discovery of errors at an early stage – but they can never replace dynamic testing.

Most programmers, asked to define testing, say something like "Testing is the process of checking a program to show there are no errors". This type of definition concentrates on errors being absent – implying that a successful test is one that shows no errors, and a failed test is one that finds an error.

However, this approach is wrong. The aim of testing is to find errors so that they can be corrected: resulting in a more reliable, and better quality final program. Thus, a better definition for testing is "The process of running software to find errors", and a successful test is one that does this rather than allowing the program to run correctly. This attitude towards testing is more likely to reveal the unreliable errors which are lurking in the program.

After all, if you use the first definition of testing, the "best" results would come from the least thorough testing; if you don't test at all, you won't find any errors in the program!

One of the most difficult questions with regard to testing is how much is enough. Although the aim of testing is to reveal errors, it is likely that some will get through the testing process without being found. Also, experience shows that, while it is fairly easy to find, say, 95% of the errors in a piece of code, it becomes more and more costly and difficult to find and correct the remaining errors. This has led to something of a compromise between what is desirable and what is achievable in terms of program correctness, and has led to a distinction between different "levels" of correctness.

The way most testing works is to input a set of values, then compare the expected results with the actual ones. If the output produced by a test run is correct, it shows the program has correctly processed that set of data. Depending on the type of data input, we can identify three levels of program correctness – possible, probable, and absolute correctness.

Possible correctness follows obtaining correct output for some arbitrary input. If the outcome of such a test is wrong, the program cannot possibly be correct.

Probable correctness involves obtaining correct output for a number of carefully selected inputs. If all potentially problematic areas are checked in this way, the program is probably correct.

Absolute correctness can be demonstrated only by a test that involves every possible combination of inputs. Such a test would take a huge amount of time; it is therefore not practicable. (However, note that, for some programs, we can prove absolute correctness using a mathematical technique known as predicate calculus. However, this is of limited use in commercial data processing.)

As a trivial example, consider the problem of testing the multiply instruction on the ICL 1900 computer. To show possible correctness, multiply 2 by 3 and check that the answer is 6. Time taken is approximately 2 microseconds.

To show probable correctness, try several values, including the obvious "problem" values such as zero, largest positive, largest negative, 1, −1, and so on. Time taken depends on the number of values used, but is of the order of a few milliseconds.

To show absolute correctness, try every possible pair of numbers. Since there are 24 bits in a 1900 word this means each operand can assume 16 777 216 different values. We cannot assume the operation is commutative, so must key all values for each operand: ie perform $16\ 777\ 216^2$ multiplications. At two microseconds per operation, this would take approximately 18 years: making no allowance for loop control or output of results!

In effect, the level of correctness required depends on how critical the application is. For programs controlling nuclear reactors or planes, for example, there is a need for absolute correctness − human life is at stake − but for many other situations it is enough to show probable correctness. Fortunately for us, we can identify the type of input data needed from the experience of other programmers in similar situations. We'll explore this in more detail later.

6.2 WHEN AND HOW?

There are three stages at which one should test a program during its development:

1 the "unit" level, testing the program modules in isolation
2 "integration" testing, testing that the linkages between each tested module work
3 "system" testing, testing the system as a whole to ensure that the component parts fit together properly.

Integration and system testing are frequently combined, especially in small scale systems in which the smallest unit is the program.

Comprehensive testing is a complex task which requires considerable planning. Since probable correctness is all that can be demonstrated, plan a sensible strategy to maximise the value of testing.

The components of a program need to be tested as they are developed, making use of available components which have already been tested. The worst way to test would be to construct all the individual components, gather them together into the final program and then commence testing. There would be so many possible sources of error in any, or all, of the components, that the only possible conclusion from the failure of such a test would be that "something has gone wrong somewhere".

The technique of de-bugging (getting rid of the bugs) requires mainly a skill in localising the source of the error. The tests need to be designed in such a way that only the section under consideration would be tested. Any errors found need to be analysed to determine whether they could appear due to a malfunction at some other point. If an amendment does not seem to be working, you are clearly looking in the wrong place. The test has failed to localise the source of the error.

A test harness

In many languages, it is not possible to test a program part by part as a program must have a given overall structure. Usually, there are many initial and final conditions to be specified, along with the special declarations and definitions regarding usage of memory and files.

In non-hierarchical program development, a specially built "test harness" is used for each component being developed. Such a harness provides the remaining structure of the program in skeleton form, thus allowing an independent test for a single component. However, it can be more wasteful in time and programmer effort to develop a harness which works. You can buy a "universal test harness" – but this sometimes results in a program being developed to suit the harness rather than the problem in hand.

On the other hand, you can develop the program in a hierarchical manner – so it becomes its own test harness. Each program component must then be functionally independent, with well defined data interfaces. "Low level utilities", such as for printing error reports, would need to be developed first; then they help in testing other, higher level components. You may also need special utilities for tasks such as inspection of files before a program can be well tested.

Using dummy stubs

It is possible, during testing for control, to pass to a component yet to be developed. Once the insertion module in Figure 6.1 is ready, one would wish to test it – though other components of the design are yet to be developed. Entering values of 2 or 3 in TRANSACTION-TYPE would lead to invalid branches in the program.

To solve this problem, each component is first replaced by a "dummy stub"; this simply announces its activation and returns control to the calling sequence. Then, as the program develops, each stub can be replaced by its actual routine.

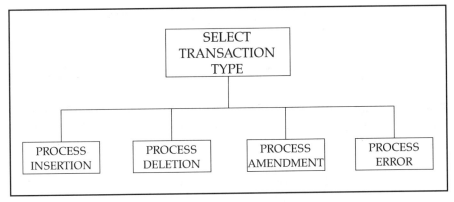

Figure 6.1   Example structure

For example, while testing the code corresponding to the following pseudocode:

```
DO CASE
    CASE transaction-type = 1
        process insertion;
    CASE transaction-type = 2
        process deletion;
    CASE transaction-type = 3
        process amendment;
ENDCASE;
```

The deletion and amendment modules would first be replaced by a dummy stub:

```
deletion:
DISPLAY "Deletion";
RETURN;
```

The program will run and report its progress. This module would be replaced with the deletion routine after testing the other parts.

Test descriptions

It is important that any tests be fully described BEFORE they are carried out. The description should include:

    a)   the identity of the component to be tested

b) the exact purpose of the test (ie which function of the component is to be tested)

c) the conditions under which the test is to be carried out (ie values of any global conditions, status of files, etc)

d) the test data to be used

e) the expected outcome (eg, new values of globals, new file statuses).

This description should be properly recorded in advance, together with a provision for recording the ACTUAL outcome of the test. Remember that anyone who carries out a test run without first describing the expected outcome is not testing, but experimenting.

It is best to draw up the test descriptions for a component as the component is being designed. By concentrating on both design and test simultaneously, you will soon realise that this gives you another chance to check the consistency of your design. Also you will find it easier to specify test data if you do this at a higher level of the design activity. On the other hand, at this stage you may merely specify the kind and range of test data, leaving the generation of actual values until later.

6.3 UNIT TESTING

Unit testing is the testing of small units of code – ie, program, module, procedure – using data designed to establish that they carry out the intended functions.

Choosing the most suitable values for test data is often not an easy task. Maybe as a result, it does not always receive the attention it deserves. Indeed, any form of testing often seems to be seen as an afterthought, rather than as an integral part of program development.

The first, and most obvious, point to make is that no sensible test data can be specified unless the exact purpose of the test is properly understood. Basically, there are two main facets of the program to be tested: the control structure and the computation.

In order to test the control structure, the significance of all selection and repetition constructs must be understood and related to the data. In our earlier example, the value of transaction type, T (an integer), could legitimately be 1, 2, or 3. Obviously any sensible test must try each of these values. In addition erroneous values, both larger and smaller, must be tried; hence the suggested test data set of 0, 1, 2, 3, 4. This is both necessary and sufficient to test all aspects of the code for SELECT TRANSACTION TYPE. There is no point in trying out the process with further values of T in this case.

Note that, when you are testing repetition constructs, take care to include a test of zero repetitions of a loop (if this is possible).

To test the computation aspects of a component, you must understand any formulas and equations used in the derivation of the algorithm – well enough to be able to appreciate the significance of data values.

Check any formula which involves multiplication with values other than 0 and 1, since you can predict the result of multiplying by each of these. For example, testing the expression $(1 - 3r)(1 + 2n)$ will give a correct-looking result if both r and n have the value 0 – even if wrongly coded with either of the signs changed or with the r typed as an n.

Similarly, terms involving exponentiation (powers) may give misleading correct results if tested with inappropriate values. Consider the formula used to calculate the periodic repayment of a mortgage loan (Figure 6.2).

$$P = \frac{A \times \frac{r}{100} \times \left(1 + \frac{r}{100}\right)^n}{\left(1 + \frac{r}{100}\right)^n - 1}$$

(A = capital sum, r = %age rate of interest, n = number of years
P = annual payments)

Figure 6.2   Mortgage loan repayment

To test an implementation of this formula we would have to run the program with selected values of A, r and n – and check the outcome with our hand-calculated result. Clearly the choice $A = 50000$, $r = 11.25$, $n = 27$ would make the hand calculation rather tedious. A better, simpler choice would be $A = 10000$, $r = 10$, $n = 2$. Take care, though, not to be too simple-minded in your choice. The set of values $A = 1000$, $n = 1$, $r = 50$ would give the correct output for the wrongly-encoded version of Figure 6.3.

$$P = \frac{A \times \frac{r}{100} \times \left(1 + \frac{r}{100}\right)^n}{\left(1 - \frac{r}{100}\right)^n + 1}$$

Figure 6.3   Wrong version of mortgage loan repayment

Also ensure that the values of all of the variables are unique – or you may fail to detect an error due to mistyping an *r* as an *n*, for instance.

Approaches to unit testing

Unit testing should take place after the code has been produced, but before any integration or system testing. In general, the amount of testing needed seems to vary with the size and complexity of the module being tested. Unfortunately, the number of defects tends to increase even faster with module size. Unit testing can, however, be made easier by designing units with high cohesion, ie having only one function. When this is the case, fewer tests are needed, and the causes of errors and methods of solution can be identified and found more easily.

There are two complementary approaches to unit testing, called black box testing and white box testing. Black box testing is where the test data is derived solely from the external specifications of the module being tested. The tester views the module as a "black box", and says "I don't care what the code looks like, or whether my tests have executed every statement in the code. As long as the coding behaves exactly as stated in the program specification, I'm happy". The ultimate testing goal is to test every possible combination and value of desired input.

In contrast, white box testing concentrates on trying to create test data which causes every instruction in the code to be executed at least once. The ultimate goal is to check every logical path in the unit – but in order to do this, the test cases have to be designed with little regard for the original code specifications.

Neither approach can, on its own, indicate unit correctness. As described earlier (in the example of multiplying two numbers), complete black box testing is impractical due to the effort required. Unfortunately, the same is true of comprehensive white box testing. Consider this COBOL 85 example.

```
LOOPING.
  PERFORM int-1 TIMES.
    IF C1
      THEN
        IF C2
          THEN
            A
          ELSE
            B
```

```
        END-IF
            ELSE
            IF C3
                THEN
                    C
                ELSE
                    D
            END-IF
        END-IF
    END-PERFORM
```

Suppose that the in-line code is to run between 1 and 10 times, the value being passed during execution; then the number of possible paths through the code will be as follows:

(a) If int-1 = 1, there are four possible paths: one corresponding to each of A,B,C, and D.

If the code is run twice: A,B,C or D can be executed the first time, along with any combination of A,B,C, or D the second time – effectively creating 4^2 possible paths.

(b) In fact the total number of possible paths through the code is:
$$4+4^2+4^3+4^4 \ldots 4^{1}0.$$

This is a geometric progression, so we can apply the formula:

$$S_n = \frac{a(r^n-1)}{r-1}$$

where a=4, being the first number in the series;
r=4, being the number of possible paths per iteration (common ratio);
n=10, being the number of iterations.

This gives the answer 4^{10}, or one million possible paths. If this simple piece of code has a million paths, testing all paths for more realistic programs is, like black box testing, impossible.

If the two extremes of the testing spectrum are both impossible, we must pick a point between them that ensures integration of the two approaches. The most practical way to do this is to concentrate on the black box aspects during testing, and leave the white box aspects to be covered by inspections, walk throughs, and similar activities. If this is not acceptable, the code has to be "instrumented" – that is, have statements added to indicate where the logical flow has gone, eg print "block 50 executed".

As well as "functional" tests, which are the ones which involve running the code with input values for which expected results are known, we have to include:

- stress tests, which involve abnormal frequencies or volumes of input, and/or abnormally high and low values
- regression tests, which compare the output from two or more test cases to ensure that the differences are as expected
- error handling tests – checking that error trapping, reporting and recovery procedures are correct.

6.4 INTEGRATION TESTING

Integration testing follows on from unit testing, it tries to identify situations where:

- data is lost between modules
- one module creates a fault in another module
- a combination of modules produces an undesirable major side effect.

There are three basic strategies here:

- top down
- bottom up
- sandwich integration.

With the top down strategy, the integration of a module starts with the main control module, and involves adding subordinate modules one at a time. The use of stubs (as explained earlier) makes the process relatively uncomplicated, but used excessively means that little or no data flows back to the main module. Other advantages include: the main control module interfaces are tested first and most often; the upper level routines provide test harnesses for the lower level ones automatically; and errors are localised, only being caused when a new module is added.

Bottom up integration starts from the lowest module and works upwards, thus avoiding the need for stubs. The big disadvantage of the method is that test harnesses have to be created for each module, which can account for 50% or more of the total effort. As integration moves up the structure, however, fewer are required at each level.

Sandwich integration is a combination of the two techniques: whereby the higher levels are tested top down, whilst the lower are tested bottom up. This reduces the need for creating test harnesses, simplifies the process and allows data to flow from the lower level modules back up to the top as it would in the real system.

6.5 SYSTEM TESTING

This type of testing checks whether the new programs operate as a coherent working system which conforms to its original specification. Testing is implemented as a black box, with examples of actual data being input to the system to check that all the functions and features conform to the specification. In addition to functional and stress tests, system testing should include:

- user interface tests, to check that the screens, prints, etc conform to the user documentation
- security tests, to check that the system is adequately protected
- recovery tests, to be sure that recovery is properly performed when the system stops abnormally
- error exit tests, to ensure that, after an error has been discovered, the message is passed through the system and that there is a tidy error exit
- help tests, to check that any help information is correct and enough.

6.6 BUGS AND DE-BUGGING

A bug is the name for an error – anything that goes wrong with your precious program when it runs. De-bugging, of course, is squashing the bugs so they cause no more trouble. Because we have carefully recorded in advance the expected outcome of each test, error identification is more simple – but still not trivial. If a test run produces an unexpected outcome, this indicates there is an error somewhere. Unfortunately, a correct outcome does not necessarily indicate that there are no errors. Careful choice of test data prevents certain kinds of errors from persisting (as indicated earlier), but it may still be possible for two or more errors to "cancel out", so the final outcome appears correct. There is no "magic formula" to ensure this has not happened – but recognising the possibility should help you guard against it when devising your test strategy.

Once you spot an error, the next task is to locate its cause. Of course if a systematic approach has been adopted throughout, this should not be too difficult. Remember that if, after a change (such as adding a new component), a program which used to work no longer seems to do so, the obvious part to examine first is the latest alteration.

Since our program does not work, we are now into the area of programming known as de-bugging. In many ways, this is the most interesting part of programming – it involves a lot of detective work which, provided it works, can be very rewarding.

A well-known saying applies to finding errors: "If you can't find what you are looking for, you are looking in the wrong place". By adopting a systematic and hierarchical approach to the development of your programs, you will achieve a certain amount of error confinement. By making components of a program as independent as possible, particularly as regards access to globally defined data items, the effects of any errors will more likely be kept to the component in which they occur.

Thus it should be fairly straight forward to find an error on the failure of a particular component test. However, we must be careful to avoid a false sense of security. Remember that when the driver of the car in front gives a hand signal, there is only one thing of which you can be absolutely sure – the window is open! Do not be misled by the apparent nature of an error indication.

How, then, to get rid of the bugs? When test data produces incorrect output, it is necessary to trace through the logic to find out how and where the program has failed. You can examine the values of memory variables by introducing additional PRINT or DISPLAY statements at selected points. Then use some variation of the dry run to trace through the code and see how these values are being produced. At the end, ensure that you remove such statements added for de-bugging purposes properly after the error has been corrected.

On inspecting the code, a few pointers may be helpful.

a) It is important to be able to approach the code with a fresh and open mind, even when looking at it for the nth time. Never believe even yourself; it is surprising how easy it is to make assumptions. The code must be seen from the viewpoint of an obedient and "dumb'" (highly literal) computer.

b) Only the output of a program is relevant while analysing a failure. The error in the output is a direct indication of what has failed, and however impossible it may seem at first (or even second) glance, the error must exist at a relevant point.

c) In case of an elusive error, keep in mind that an error can escalate and show up at a point far from where it was caused. The total picture must, therefore, be re-examined at such times.

d) It sometimes helps to be able to "image" the problem, especially when it is connected with one of the input or output devices or with a file transfer. While considering each statement, try to imagine exactly what would be happening on the computer in response.

Once you have found an error, you must correct it. Take care to avoid the application of purely arbitrary changes to the code, accompanied by cries of "let's see what this does!". By carefully working through the code with test data, you should satisfy yourself that you know exactly how the incorrect result arose, and from that, how to alter the code to correct the error.

Refer to the data dictionary to ensure that data items are still being used properly. Once a correction has been formulated, perform a careful desk check before re-checking the program using the original test data.

Errors naturally fall into two classes: logic errors and coding errors. Logic errors should be trapped and corrected before the program is encoded and tested. If, possibly owing to a misunderstanding (but probably due to carelessness), a test fails owing to a logical error, the programmer must re-examine the logic at the highest possible level to correct the fault. Though it may appear easier to "juggle the code" to correct the problem, this must be avoided as it does not solve the problem – it merely evades it. Take care to document any alteration to the logic of the program, and to make adequate checks to guard against the introduction of new errors by inconsistent use of data items.

Coding errors will not occur very often if you adopt a systematic approach. When they do occur, they almost invariably follow a misuse of the language facilities. This is usually due to an inadequate understanding of, or familiarity with, the language in use. All programmers should ensure they understand fully all aspects of the languages they use, rather than "muddle through'" using a sometimes inappropriate subset.

So that you may more readily detect the cause of a program's failure, be able to make effective use of all the clues provided. In addition, you must be able to take the necessary steps to provide as many clues as possible.

The operating system offers a number of utilities you will find useful when trying to debug a program. Thus, while testing a program which generates or changes the contents of a file, it is necessary to be able to examine the contents. Similarly, it helps if you can examine the contents of selected memory variables while the program is running or at the point where it fails. That is what various utility programs are for.

Earlier utilities would offer a facility to "dump" the contents of the file and memory in a general octal or hexadecimal format, that is, they would print out the characters without any attempt to interpret them. The programmer had to trace painstakingly through all this code, trying to derive the required information. By referring to compiler and linker listings, and using octal or hexadecimal arithmetic, it was possible to work out the addresses of the required storage cells. The data would then be interpreted.

Nowadays the symbolic de-buggers and program tracers make this kind of effort unnecessary. There is generally a file examination utility which prints or displays a file serially using a general code like ASCII. A de-bugger package accepts built in checkpoints where the program execution halts (with the program store left intact) and allows memory examination. The memory addresses corresponding to each variable can be determined using the cross-reference table provided.

A "trace" package, offered by most compilers and interpreters, lets you watch program runs by displaying the name of the module or the number of the statement being carried out from moment to moment. Some packages also let you specify certain variables, which are then displayed whenever their values change.

Most reasonable batch operating systems automatically record major events on a system "log" file. Such information as which files have been opened and/or closed and the number of file transfers appear here. Some systems can even log the number of instructions executed, together with a list of the last N (typically 16) instructions. This sort of information can be very useful when you are trying to reconstruct the sequence of events which led to a program failure.

Today's third and fourth generation languages generally provide many more facilities for debugging. Along with trace packages, there are facilities for "single stepping" through the program – carrying it out one step at a time, with examination of storage cells as required.

A facility called "animation" displays source code at run time, highlighting the current instruction as it is executed. You can combine this facility with single stepping to get single step with animation.

Many languages let you inspect the variables called by name when the program has stopped. Not only is the storage space saved, but the variable names can be made to retain their meaning when outside the program.

Perhaps the greatest danger involved with interactive de-bugging is that of the unrecorded fix. There is a great temptation, having made the program work, to forget to update the documentation. All that is required is adequate self-discipline – easy to say, but not so easy to achieve. If you are working in an interactive environment remember to save the latest working version of your program and to destroy all out-of-date versions. Also, when editing the source program, remember to record the version number correctly in the source.

NOW TRY THESE . . .

Exercise One

a) What are the two main types of testing called?

b) Name the three levels of correctness, and explain why it is not likely that the highest of these can be achieved in practice.

7 Implementation

OBJECTIVES

When you have worked through this chapter, you should be able to:
- state what field testing is and why people need it
- compare pilot and parallel running
- explain the nature of, and need for, program maintenance
- list some of the questions a program review should consider.

INTRODUCTION

Once the programmer has properly finished developing, coding and testing the program, the task is almost over. Now the project team will release the program to play its part in the overall system — the programmer has just some tidying up to do.

How the team will release the program depends on the installation. In most cases, however, the process will involve some kind of acceptance test; this must take place to the satisfaction of the user (or representative). Sometimes the project team will carry out the acceptance testing — more often not. In any event, the programmer will have to provide enough information to allow a proper acceptance test.

Of course, the programmer (or the team as a whole) should have produced adequate documentation — this will include details of program testing, with full notes on test data used and the results. Many users will agree that those records are enough to show that the program is acceptable. On the other hand, some wish to provide a new set of test data; in that case, the team runs the program with the new data, checking output and documenting the process as before.

The standard of user documentation is, of course, a major aspect of the acceptability of a program package. Often programmers are not involved in producing this (perhaps it is part of the original specification), but they should clearly be familiar with its form and contents.

As well as user documentation, the released program needs an operations manual. This may be part of the user manual or separate from it. Often the programmer will have made some input to this document, perhaps giving details of the run-time messages the program provides.

145

I don't go into detail on the above matters here — you need to know about them, though, for they are part of the general picture. In particular, we come to documentation in Chapter 9. Rather, now we deal with implementation — the process of taking a finished program and using it in practice.

The program's implementation itself normally involves a programme of field trials, in a sense part of the acceptance testing. We look at aspects of that in this chapter. We also consider the field of program review and maintenance — what people do to keep the program up to date in the light of changed needs once it is running in final form.

7.1   RUNNING IN THE FIELD

Experience shows that the best way to discover what is wrong with one's software is to let other people use it. Some embarrassment may be avoided if the initial release of a program takes the form of a field trial release. This involves the cooperation of the users – you are asking them to try out the program "warts and all", and to report back any difficulties.

Field trials usually take one of four forms.

(a)   The most common is parallel running, in which the data continues to be processed by the existing system – perhaps a manual system – and is also processed, in parallel, by the new system which incorporates your programs. The results are then compared, and after satisfactory results have been obtained from the new system for a period of time, the results of the new system are actually used – and shortly after, the old system lapses.

Parallel running, of course, not only requires the user to provide extra effort to run both systems, but also involves effort in comparing the results of the two systems. This is the real life test – because the expected results are (usually) the results of the old system.

(b)   Instead of this, the user may accept the testing that has been done as adequate proof of correctness, and to change over directly to the new system – people often call this "sudden death". Some user environments require that type of change over – and the testing needs to be even more rigorous and detailed in such circumstances.

The other approaches are to do pilot or phased installation.

(c)   Pilot installation is when a small group of users work with the new system, leaving the bulk of the users to operate the old one. As confidence is gained, more and more users change to the new system – over a period of time.

Phased installation usually involves all the users at once, but with only part of the system – other parts being introduced when the previous part has settled down. An illustration of this last could be the introduction first of stock recording, followed by forecasting of forward demand, then automatic order progress and full stock control, and finally automatic ordering as well as everything else.

In any case, the programmer may eventually receive some feedback as to how the system performed in practice, together with requests for amendments or enhancements. Since this feedback may not come for many months after the hand over of the program, the importance of unambiguous, concise and complete documentation is clear.

If the program is to replace part or all of an existing computer system, the programmer may well also be involved in the provision of special routines for file conversion and file set-up. These additional demands should, of course, have been specified with the system – but the programmer must be prepared for errors in changeover runs and even late-notice extensions and changes in requirements. Such problems will often require some emergency action, especially if a live deadline is at stake.

7.2 MAINTENANCE

All programs require maintenance. As far as users are concerned, the most important aspect of computing is running programs and keeping their performance in line with corporate requirements. Program maintenance – keeping the programs up to date with real user needs – is straight forward then.

Unfortunately it seems that many data processing professionals do not see things this way. For them, computing is about the challenge of developing new systems and using the latest technology. That view can make program maintenance much more of a problem.

There are two major problems associated with program maintenance. First, many programmers seem to dislike the work, being more interested in planning and designing their own solutions to problems. Secondly, as programs are often large and complex structures, they can be difficult to change. It is almost always easier for a program's authors to change it than anyone else, but this means constantly interrupting their current work.

One solution is to separate program development work from maintenance, although this is very much dependent upon the number and type of staff available.

Whatever structure is employed, any programmer can expect to be involved in the maintenance of programs at some time or other. Bearing this in mind, good advice is to "do as you would be done by": in other words, produce programs which anyone else can maintain, because you will probably have to maintain other people's programs yourself.

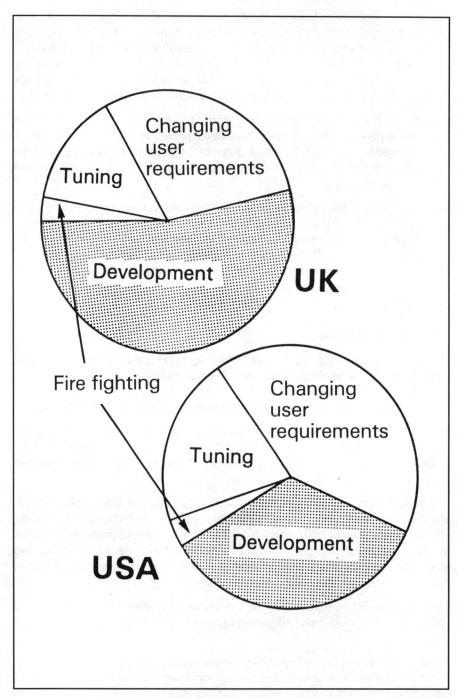

**Figure 7.1   Proportion of programming time
spent on maintenance**

Figure 7.1 shows estimates of the amount of programmer effort devoted to maintenance compared with new development. These estimates vary from 47% to as much as 80%, the higher figure being quoted in the US. Of that maintenance effort, approximately 5% is "emergency fire-fighting" (ie bug correction), 30% is efficiency improvement, and the remaining 65% is satisfying users' requests for changes.

Often this last category simply involves producing new outputs from existing files: such requests are best met by the provision of suitable user-driven software, such as FILETAB. In a way, the reason behind many of such suggestions in this book is the amount of effort that maintenance takes – and the associated costs. The factors that people find affect most the cost of program maintenance include degree of program structure, modularity, complexity, and level of documentation – all subjects covered in one way or another here.

Another justification for the techniques described is that they increase programmer productivity. This also relates to maintenance in that the DP industry has for some time suffered a "skills shortage" – a lack of trained programmers – as a result of the huge resources necessary to maintain existing computer systems. This has delayed the development of new systems and created an "applications backlog" – where not enough programmers are available to do the amount of programming needed. The adoption of better techniques, leading to increased productivity, releases skilled staff earlier to produce the new systems people require.

As far as concerns the programmer, maintenance jobs start with a specification; this describes the required changes of behaviour and refers to the program(s) concerned. Provided that the correct documentation has been filed for the program, you should experience no real difficulty in identifying which parts require change, or in working out the amount and scope of the changes needed.

Make sure that alterations are properly documented at all appropriate levels, and that an amendment history log is kept for the program; this should show who authorised each change and for what reason. It is also your responsibility to carry out the necessary re-testing, including proper testing of the amended components and a re-run of any overall confidence tests to ensure that the integrity of the system remains. Note that all the modifications and testing are done to a separate copy of the program – never to the actual version itself.

7.3 PROGRAM REVIEWS

It is normal to review the performance of any computer-based system at a set time after implementation, and, perhaps, at stated intervals thereafter. Such reviews concern the human as well as the computer activities; they may involve the user, systems, operations and programming departments.

It is wise to check all operational programs at intervals appropriate to their frequency of use. The questions to ask about each program include these below:

- Does it match up to its estimated size and performance?
- Is throughput satisfactory – can it be improved further?
- Are there any operational or interface difficulties?
- Is output in accordance with requirements? Are there any "rough edges" to smooth?
- What amendments have been made since the last review?
- How many times has emergency action been necessary since the last review?
- Is the documentation in a satisfactory state?
- What further action is recommended?

Ideally, a programmer other than the author should check an individual program. This means, of course, that the documentation of all programs must be produced to the same high standard. The maintenance and review of all programs will be much simplified if systematic methods of design and development are followed. Programmers will then realise that maintenance gives them the opportunity to extend their knowledge and understanding of user requirements, programming techniques and operational considerations.

NOW TRY THESE...

Exercise One

a)   There are four types of field trials, what are they?

b)   What are the advantages and disadvantages of each?

8   Documentation

OBJECTIVES

When you have worked through this chapter, you should be able to:

- explain the place of documentation within overall system development
- describe the need for, and the features of, good documentation
- outline the main stages of system life cycle
- state the three elements of the system flow chart
- understand and use the standard system flow chart symbols
- list the aspects of a program that the specification needs to cover
- list and describe the seven main parts of the program manual.

INTRODUCTION

Documentation, both for users and for future programmers, is a crucial part of any serious program package. It is, however, no more crucial than any other aspect of program development – and here we take the opportunity to go through the whole development process (the so called system life cycle). This is important, if for no other reason than that this is the book's last chapter on programming as a process.

8.1 WHY DOCUMENT?

Creating documentation, although sometimes a little tedious, is a very important part of a programmer's work. The purposes of documentation are:

- communication
- quality control
- reference.

Poor communication between the people involved in the development of a system causes major problems, as the information passed from phase to phase becomes distorted. Documentation is an integral part of the inspection process; it ensures that the intentions of the originator of the system survive intact from specification to design and from design to coding.

In addition it allows communication not only from stage to stage in development, but also between people involved in the same stage. Data processing is well known for high employee turnover; planned and standardised documentation reduces the impact of staff changes, and allows trained staff to move from one project to another easily.

As with any other product, software quality has to be checked at regular intervals throughout its production. As we shall see later, documentation is part of the "exit criteria" (or final output) from each stage of the production process; as such its quality reflects the quality of the specification, design and code produced. Also because it is completed at the end of each stage of production, we can use it to indicate the status of a software project – not just as a tool to assist in its management.

Lastly, the reference aspect of documentation. It is rare that any computer program remains the same for a long period. Systems change in response to changes in the business environment in which they exist, or to the discovery of errors in programs. Therefore it is likely that changes will be needed at some point. One of the most frustrating things for programmers is not to be able quickly to understand a program that they, or someone else, has coded in the past. Up to date standardised documentation enables them to do this accurately and with the minimum of effort.

What, then, makes good documentation?

8.2   GOOD DOCUMENTATION

To be useful, it is necessary that relevant data is available, correct and easy to locate. In an evolving system, although people may start with good intentions, documentation is often left incomplete. Amendments may grow faster than any records of them – and existing documents soon become out of date. The number of documents produced increases faster and faster – therefore they must be properly numbered, dated, tabulated and supplied with cross references.

In a well documented system, standards are followed by all team members; then each member understands the format and can instantly access the required information. No computer user has the time or desire to trace through complicated charts or adjust to differing styles of information presentation.

For the programmer, we can divide documentation into two parts: pre-program and post-program. Most of the pre-program documentation comes from someone else – while because the programmer is last in the production chain, that person will be responsible for producing the post-program documentation.

So far we have not considered what happens outside our program in terms of the development of the system as a whole. Since we are dealing with documentation, let us consider how to describe the whole process of system development.

In the same way that we broke down the structure of the program into more easily managed elements, we can break down the development of a complete system. The name for this description of a system is its "life cycle": so called because it charts its development from conception to maturity (and, in fact, back again).

The life cycle has a number of stages, some of which we have already met. See Figure 8.1.

1	INITIAL STUDY
2	SYSTEM DESIGN
3	PROGRAM DESIGN
4	CODING
5	TESTING
6	INSTALLATION
7	LIVE RUNNING
8	REVIEW

Figure 8.1   Life cycle stages

The user request is the first event in the cycle. Before any assessment is possible, it is necessary to have a precise definition of the requirements in a form acceptable to the analyst as well as to the user.

There are two basic reasons for ensuring that the user involvement in the requirements specification is maximised: one of these is technical, the other is psychological.

First, the technical reasons: the requirements specification fulfils two roles: firstly, it is the technical document that forms the major input into the design of the system, and secondly the contents of the requirements specification provide the baseline against which all the acceptance tests will ultimately be checked. Hence a badly designed specification will produce a system which will not meet the users needs, resulting in the need for expensive rectification later in the life cycle, (if practical) and delays in the successful introduction of the system. (See figure 8.2.)

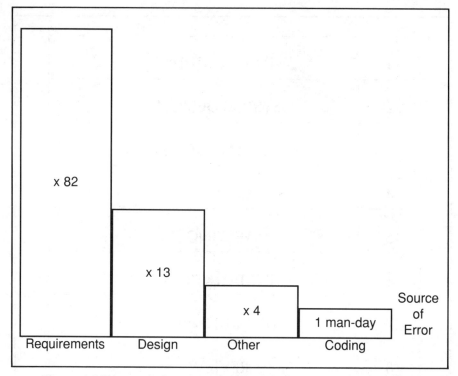

Figure 8.2 Diagram showing the relative cost of correcting errors

The requirements specification may also be used as the basis for a legal contract, which means that any disagreement over whether the system has been completed satisfactorily may have to be resolved by reference to the content.

Since the whole point of developing a system is to meet the needs of the users, it is important from a psychological point of view that they feel that they 'own' the system and that it is not being imposed on them from above or by another department.

The requirements should be specified at two levels. The higher level should be an overall summary containing an outline of the requirements, any assumptions that have been made, and a description of the development timescale. At the lower level the requirements should be expressed as functional and non-functional. The functional requirements are the processes that the system should support. These can be verified by trying the processes to see that they work, and by making sure that their opposites don't. Eventually these activities will form the basis for a set of procedural tests that will become part of the final user evaluation criteria for the system. The procedural tests should be specified for normal working conditions but in addition the events which are to be treated as exceptions should also be defined along with the degree of impairment to the system that is acceptable.

The non-functional requirements are a little more difficult to define since they relate principally to the environment in which the system will operate. Nevertheless it is essential that aspects such as performance, security, quality and flexibility should be defined in terms of actual measurements or if this is not possible in terms of subjective assessment.

The job of obtaining the necessary information to user requirements can be very difficult if the system being developed is a large one. Initially at least, information can be obtained from questionnaires and interviews. Questionnaires are often difficult to devise unless you are a specialist in the area, but they are generally cheap to distribute. Unfortunately however they sometimes alienate the recipients and the results can be difficult to interpret accurately. Interviews are more time consuming but if they are planned can provide better results.

The acid tests for the measurement of the adequacy and completeness of a requirements specification is whether someone who was not involved in the original definition, could perform the next stage of designing the system using this requirements specification. This is sometimes a necessity as the analyst is not always the same person as the designer of the system.

One important contributory factor to this is that as far as possible each requirement should be capable of only one interpretation. This is often difficult to achieve in a 'natural' language such as English.

The systems analyst tries to determine the scope of the project, the hardware involved, the time frame, the cost, the staffing needed, the benefits, and other relevant parameters – all to assess the feasibility of the project. For this task, a variety of techniques may be used. For example, there may be interviews with the end users, study of the input/output documents, and assessment of the volume of data involved. The analyst would define the requirements tentatively and modify them after further discussions with the user.

The results may go forward in the form of a proposal. Once this is accepted by the user, the next stage, system design, can start.

The analyst must now prepare detailed system specifications, spelling out the lines of information flow in the system, and designing the file storage and the documents involved. The steps to achieve this will be worked out up to a brief description of the programs. The user documentation for the system would also be outlined. If relevant, control and security procedures would be explored. In addition, a system test plan should be prepared which details the requirements that have to be met before the system can be considered operational.

When a large system is to be produced, this stage could involve a lot of activity and analysis, with an investigation being planned first and various fact finding methods being designed – such as interviews, questionnaires and general or specific observation. Many documents may be produced before this stage is over, with a filing system being used for storing and cross-referencing documents. Some prototype documents may be designed to help the user evaluate and formally approve the system.

Briefly, the existing system must be carefully studied to determine the information flow: the elements of information, and the point of origin and the destination of each. This flow is analysed to determine the needs for input documents, the files which must be maintained and the outputs of the system: queries, documents, reports and so on. Now, the analyst can define the processes and procedures: for using the given inputs to create records on files and obtain the necessary outputs from these.

To computerise the system, the hardware, the personnel, the lines of information flow and each of the above elements must be designed and optimised. Every element must be fully defined, and the procedures are broken into a set of programs: with one for each discrete activity, such as, perhaps, setting up a file, entering or editing data, querying data, and producing each of the outputs.

Other aspects of the analysis may include specification of staffing and time schedules, defining stages, and planning and laying down procedures for user interaction, user involvement, and user training.

Events in a system – òr part of a system – were traditionally represented diagrammatically by means of a system flow chart. This is one of the end products of the system design stage.

The system flow chart shows three elements: the programs, the data, and their interaction. It is similar to a program run chart. Although still used by many analysts, it has several disadvantages as an aid to viewing a system. In particular, it may be created after the programs and other elements have been designed – and this may not be the best approach.

These charts are now giving way to the data flow diagrams (DFD) at different levels, to the LDS (logical data structure) and to the ELH (entity life history). These may be used during the system design stage, and the most important is the DFD.

The DFD illustrates the data movement in the system. It shows the flow of information to, from, and within a system. There is generally no provision for showing conditional actions within these diagrams. All possible flows appear, while decisions are made within the processes themselves.

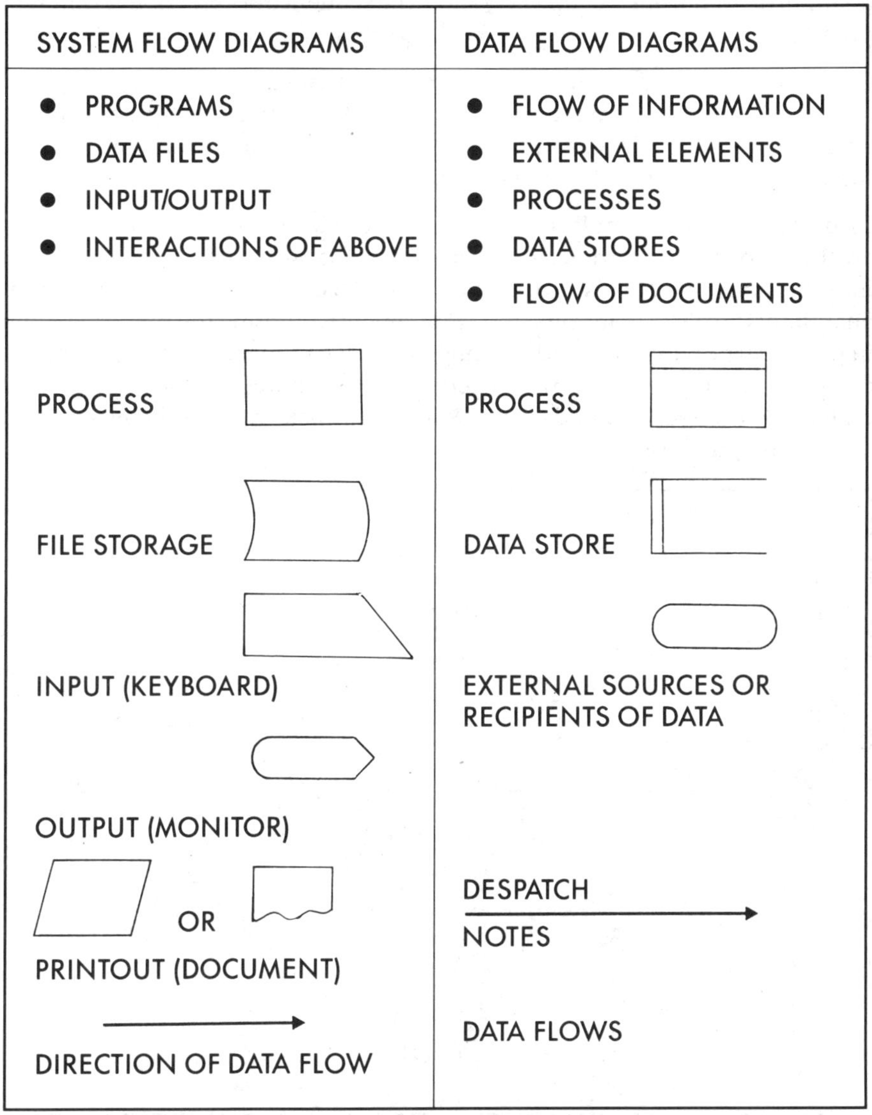

SYSTEM FLOW DIAGRAMS	DATA FLOW DIAGRAMS
• PROGRAMS • DATA FILES • INPUT/OUTPUT • INTERACTIONS OF ABOVE	• FLOW OF INFORMATION • EXTERNAL ELEMENTS • PROCESSES • DATA STORES • FLOW OF DOCUMENTS
PROCESS FILE STORAGE INPUT (KEYBOARD) OUTPUT (MONITOR) OR PRINTOUT (DOCUMENT) DIRECTION OF DATA FLOW	PROCESS DATA STORE EXTERNAL SOURCES OR RECIPIENTS OF DATA DESPATCH NOTES DATA FLOWS

Figure 8.3 Flow diagrams

The symbols used are in Figure 8.3. Elements from outside the system are shown by an oval, a process is a rectangle with a division within it for cross-referencing and numbering. A file or data store is named and numbered in a thinner rectangle, while labelled arrows show the direction of data flow. The labels indicate the item of data which is moving.

We write program or procedure names in rectangles – with the inputs, outputs and backing storage elements, along with their names, shown for each. Each file appears only once, and arrows link it to those programs which use it either for input or for output. Arrows also show the sequence of execution of different programs.

The chart of a large system is broken down so that sub-units of it can appear on different pages. In this case, it may be necessary to show the same file or program more than once. Appropriate reference numbers and symbols must then aid cross-referencing as required.

Figure 8.4 gives an example of a DFD for part of a purchasing system. Two files are involved: a stock file and a purchase orders file. Received goods are entered into the stock file; this is processed to order parts. Ordering consists of an analysis of the file to determine the requirements, entering the purchase order in the corresponding file, and printing out purchase orders for the suppliers. Suppliers, in turn, provide the material along with delivery notes which are entered by the receive-goods process into the stock file, after being checked against the purchase orders.

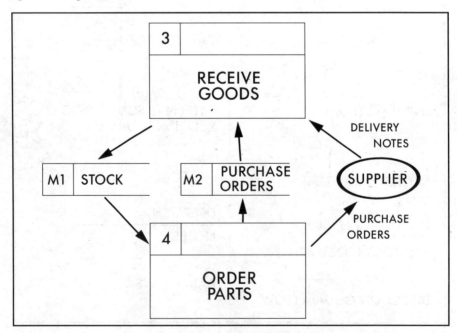

Figure 8.4 Example DFD

The system flow diagram corresponding to the above system is shown in Figure 8.5.

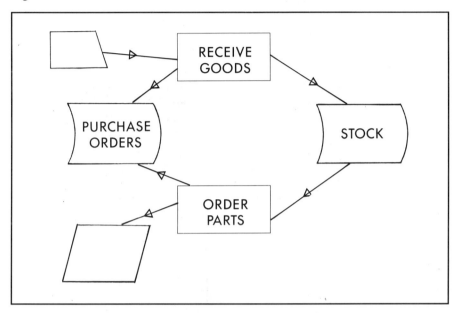

Figure 8.5 System flow diagram

A part of a purchase system is shown here. There are two programs and two files. The receive-goods procedure uses the purchase-orders file as input and accepts delivery details from the keyboard. It writes stock-details onto the stock file. The stock file provides input to the order-parts program which outputs data to the purchase-orders file and prints out purchase orders.

Program design

After that side track into the basics of systems analysis, we can return to program documentation. Our concern now is program specification. After the systems analyst has designed the system, a senior member of the programming staff designs the programs. It may be found that some of the programs already exist. If a system's requirements can be met by an existing program, the senior programmer may liaise with systems staff to alter the specifications to fit with this.

Test procedures would be laid down by the analyst and there would be a number of constraints within which the program must run.

Programs are now assigned to various programmers. Working from the specifications, the programmer produces a detailed program design and a test schedule for each program. These may be checked out by a senior colleague before coding commences.

System Outline NCC	Title	System	Document	Name	Sheet
	Sales Order Processing	*SOP*	*3·1*	*SOPSYS*	*1*

Inputs

Customer Order Details
Customer Alteration to Order Details
Data Preparation Control Sheet
Order Input File
New Orders and Alterations
Order Controls
Despatch Detail Input File

Processes

Clerical Order Entry
Clerical Alteration to Customer Orders
Order File Data Preparation
Computer Order Acknowledgement
Clerical Sales Order Despatch
→ Sales Order Despatch Data Preparation
Computer Despatch
Clerical Order Batching

Files

Customer Index
Product Catalogue
Customer Card Library
Product Card Library
Outstanding Orders
Doubtful Credit List
Delivery Cost List
Factory Stock List
Product Order Book
Factory Order Ledger

Outputs

Order Acknowledgement
Advice/Consignment Note
Balance Order
Invoice Details Tape

Notes, cross references

S 31

Author	Issue
	Date

© 1969. The National Computing Centre Limited

Figure 8.6 S31 System outline form

Coding, with appropriate standards being used, and implementation are sometimes handled by junior programmers. This stage is followed by testing. Throughout all stages program documentation must be prepared according to the agreed standards. The contents of the program specification are shown below:

- the inputs to the program
- the outputs from the program
- the major program functions
- the way the program interfaces with the program before and the program after it
- the parameters for any utility programs that are used (such as sort sequence and sort keys for a sort program)
- the validation requirements for input data
- the requirements for the layout of output data printout and screens
- the action to be taken on errors and exceptions
- any special requirements for tables, formulas or algorithms.

As well as a list of the major program functions the specification may also contain a more detailed description of the logical rules and decisions the program must involve, and more details about how the input should be checked, altered and used.

Sometimes the program specification is contained in a set of formal documents. Figure 8.5 shows a system outline form (S31): part of the NCC Data Processing Documentation Standards. This is one of an integrated set of documents which covers the whole system life cycle – but they are not the only way to document the program specification. The others follow the same theme, however (see Figure 8.6).

Sometimes (but rarely) the specifications are "free form", that is without any pre-defined standard format. The benefits to be gained from well designed documentation are well known, and we have come a long way from the time when program specifications were written informally on scraps of paper.

Finally the systems analyst will supply a systems test plan, containing details of:

- test organisation
- scheduling
- test cases.

Test organisation would include the test objectives, who was responsible for what, and details of any existing files used in the testing of other systems.

The schedule then lists the sequence of the tests, the input files needed, and the expected results. It describes each test case separately, and includes details of the input format and the output expected, and precisely what is being tested.

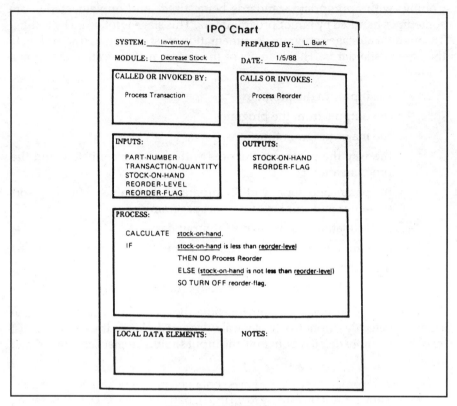

Figure 8.7 IPO chart

In Chapter 6, we began by describing the testing of individual modules of code, then moved to integration testing and finally system testing. This document describes the tests to be undertaken at the highest of these levels: system testing; later the programmer must prepare a similar test plan for the program modules.

So far we have defined the programming tasks as follows:

- logic analysis
- coding
- desk checking
- test data preparation
- compilation and testing.

Now we will see how the documentation produced by the programmer fits in with each of these stages, and ties them all together.

The program specification and systems test plan will be given to a programmer to code. The programmer uses the documentation as the source of the information needed to design and code the program. The framework most often used to bring together all the components of the final product is the program manual. This goes to the user, and should contain the items following. Study this before we look at the items in more detail:

- a general description of the program – its function, use, and methodology
- descriptions of the program input, files and output
- structure charts showing the logic
- descriptions of any messages output
- code
- test plan
- testing and operating instructions.

8.3 INSIDE THE PROGRAM MANUAL

In the program description, one must be careful to include the identification of the program – and it is useful to have data regarding the date of completion, the author, the machine and peripherals expected to be used, as well as of the constraints under which the program works or any quality criteria which it must meet.

During installation of the system, there are often special procedures required such as first time initialisation of files, options and system parameters. If the system is to replace an out-dated software system, the files on computer may need to be converted so as to be compatible with the new one. If it is a computerisation of a manual system, all hand-written data needs to be converted into files on backing store. Any special procedures associated with the installation of the program need to be described. (Some programs, for example, may be run at one site only.)

The error codes, messages used and actions taken also appear in the user's manual.

If the program runs independently, it will be necessary to specify the instructions to be given to the operating system to enable a user to run the program. If the running is handled by the system, the job control instructions to be included in the batch file will be specified.

Restricted use and security measures are imposed on some programs. The kind of authorisation required may also be specified.

There should also be a description of the program, containing the equivalent information to that included in the program specification, as well as information about:

- special hardware or equipment needed
- subroutines used
- special formulas, eg for random number generation
- other specialised information not recorded anywhere else.

The data specification should also be equivalent to the description on the program specification – but, in addition, if the programmer is responsible for developing the layouts, samples of these should appear too.

To provide the necessary information on program logic, include hierarchy charts along with the pseudocode developed from them.

Program listings

With the high cost of program maintenance, good documentation can be justified solely as an aid to later modification. Although most installations insist that the program manual is kept up to date, updating is (more often than not) done after the event. As a result, there are sometimes differences between the listing and the rest of the manual.

However it is usually the listing that the programmer first looks at when considering modifying or amending the program, so this should be considered as the front line of documentation, and as the most credible of the documents.

Since clarity is the main objective, the way that the program has been coded should be reflected in the listings. Examples of the ways to achieve this follow:
- introductory comments to indicate program and programmer identification, date of compilation, and so on
- layout of that part of the program in which the data is defined, such that
    - there is a sequence in the declaration of input/output areas, work areas, tables, constants, messages, etc
    - data names appear both meaningful and consistent with a standard pattern
    - comments explain the purpose and use of fields
- layout of the program in terms of blocks, their identification labels, and the spacing between them
- the format of source statement so that the logical structure is apparent from their indentation
- use of comments to describe the processing part of the program.

When the documentation is for the benefit of the programmer, the best approach may be to incorporate as much as possible in the source code. Programmers tend to maintain the source code, and as they change the code are more likely to update the comments to match, rather than redrawing flowcharts or other external documents. Another advantage is that if the documentation is closely allied to the code, then the code can be checked against the specification easily and almost simultaneously, thus making any coding errors obvious.

Next, the program test plan should comprise:
- as many of the test methods as possible, and a note of the sequence of application of the tests

- a list of the test cases, subdivided into purpose, input, and expected output for each one
- a listing of the test data.

Each test case should be numbered and described in its own subsection – then the test plan can act as a control document, recording the number of tests, types of error and so on. As an example, Figure 8.8 shows NCC document S34 in which the test details have been compiled into a decision table. Figure 8.9 shows a test plan.

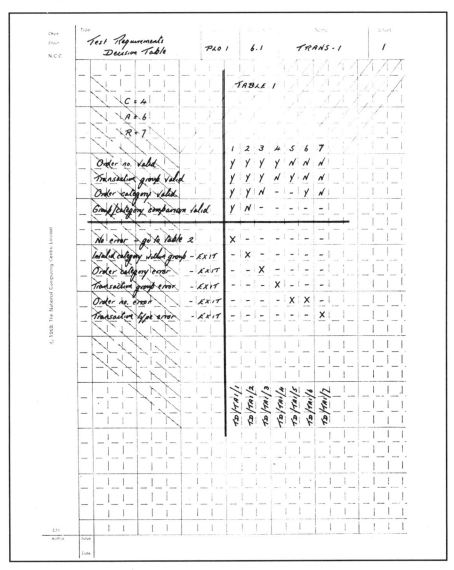

Figure 8.8 Test requirements decision table

Test no	Purpose	Included with test	Test result	No of shots	Start	Finish
1	Compilation	—	Error-free listing	P 3	2/6/77	4/6/77
2	Sample data: no errors	PRO1/TACON : Tested / PRO1/KPROM : Test h	'No errors' report / diagnoses TRANS-1/3/2.2	P 3	3/6/77	9/6/77
3	* To BOSH only when Test 2 is complete / Comprehensive error data	as above with KPROM test s	D.T. msg: TRANS-VI; TRANS-1/2 data spec TA1	P 4	10/6/77	12/6/77
4	Corrupt header data	PRO1/TACON	ABANDON Run "INVALID BATCH"	P 1	14/6/77	16/6/77

Test Plan NCL — Title: TRANS-1 Test — System: PRO 1 — Document: 6.2 — Name: TRANS-1 — Sheet: 4

S51 — Author — Issue — Date

© 1972 The National Computing Centre Limited

Figure 8.9 Test plan

At installation, the program is released to take its place in the system, and the programmer's work is nearly over. Installation may involve many one time activities, such as first initialisation of parameters, creation or conversion of files, and so on. After this is done, some form of acceptance tests have to be conducted, to satisfy the users or their representative. This is not, generally, done by the programmers, but as discussed already, their documentation must be complete to enable an outsider to perform the tests.

8.4 USER DOCUMENTATION

Manuals produced as user documentation can vary widely in quality; but they should not be undervalued as they can be very important in determining the popularity and lifetime of a system, no matter how well developed the rest is. Thus, it is good to invest a lot of imagination and care in this activity, and the programmer may be expected to contribute.

Depending on the size of the system, the user guide may be a small pamphlet, a booklet or a number of manuals. A guide may describe the system, its strategies, facilities, and application areas, as well as run time instructions. In the current environment of interactive, menu-driven systems, the operating instructions need to be given according to the user activity desired, rather than program by program as normally produced by a programmer.

In the case of a program produced to be sold, documentation may also be required by the marketing department. This would cover, briefly, the salient points of the package, how it differs from other packages on the market, and the type of people that would be interested.

Programmers are not generally involved in production of user documentation. However, they need to be able to point out special features in the programs they write.

NOW TRY THESE...

Exercise One

    a) List the stages of the system life-cycle.

    b) What criticisms can you make about this model?

9 Program languages and operating software

OBJECTIVES

When you have worked through this chapter, you should be able to:

- list and explain the four main features used for comparing program languages
- state in each case a number of attributes of a "good" program language
- explain, with examples, what we mean by saying a high level program language is application-oriented
- provide an outline description of COBOL, FORTRAN, BASIC, PASCAL and C
- demonstrate some understanding of actual code in each case
- explain the need for, and outline the nature of, program standards
- state why dialects are common and why we are currently far from a universal program language
- put those points within the context of the history of program languages
- state what operating software is, and outline the major types
- outline the main tasks of operating software.

INTRODUCTION

So far we've almost entirely avoided details of specific program languages. That's because programming is an activity that involves a great many concepts and skills that are quite language-independent – but now we've explored those concepts and skills in detail.

Having done that, it's important for you to be able to compare program languages in the light of those general needs. In this chapter we see how to do that by looking briefly at some examples. We also see that even languages which offer the basic structures and allow the basic skills (which not all do) still vary a great deal as regards other useful features.

In fact, comparing program languages is far from easy. A major reason for this is that, like human languages, they evolve – in fact, most change very fast with time. (Not only do standards change, but system-specific dialects are common.) It is also very hard to be objective – all programmers have their favourite languages.

These points have their roots in history. Therefore, in this chapter we take the opportunity to put the development of program languages – and that of operating software – into an historical context. What will the future bring?

9.1   ESSENTIAL LANGUAGE FEATURES

The aims of a program language are to ease:

- the clear and precise development of computer programs
- communication between programmers and computers
- communication between programmers and other people.

That being so, we can describe, under four main headings, those features which are essential if the language is to be at all useful. They are:

- data description
- data manipulation
- data communication (input/output – I/O)
- sequence control.

We shall now look at each of these in turn.

Data description

The language must allow the programmer to describe the data involved in a problem in a useful manner. As an absolute minimum this should allow the use of labels that are meaningful (to the programmer) to stand for items of data. The programmer should also be able, when specifying each data label, to indicate the kind of information involved (eg, numeric or non-numeric, fixed or floating point). Also, ideally, we should be able to give a possible range of values in each case.

The design of successful solutions to information processing problems is both simpler and safer if the language includes facilities which enable the programmer to describe the data in a problem oriented way.

Since most problems involve numeric information, most computer languages include facilities for representing numbers. Usually, however, there are only two kinds of numeric data type available: integers (whole) and floating point (real) numbers. Within most languages there are no facilities for restricting the range of values which may be stored in any particular variable; as a result, there are no built in run time checks for unexpected (invalid) input values.

When you declare a variable, the ability to specify the allowed range of values lets you take full advantage of any run time range checks. If, in addition, the language lets you associate your own labels with sub-ranges of values, the compiler can offer still further consistency checks. This allows reporting of any misuse of data ranges at translation time.

In many programs, numbers can stand for information which is really non-numeric in nature: such as days of the week, positions within a firm, named stock levels. The construction and maintenance of programs is much eased by the use of language features which enable, for example, the use of named constants or, better still, non-numeric scalar (discrete) data types. Such features are only now coming to be generally available, but we must hope that their use will spread.

In addition to the use of discrete data items, many problems involve data which is tabular or structured in some other way. Obviously, in order to construct programs to solve such problems, we must be able to represent those structures.

The simplest form of structured data is the vector or linear (one-dimensional) array; this is closely followed in value by the matrix or rectangular (two-dimensional) array. Most languages support arrays of one or two dimensions (some even for higher orders) – but usually only for use with numeric data. The languages which offer arrays of non-numeric data often restrict all the elements of an array to the same data type. This can lead to our having to use either several arrays for what is essentially a single data structure or some non-natural data encoding (such as holding numbers as digit strings) – in order to allow a single structure. A desirable feature of a program language would be arrays of elements that differ in type. In this way we could show a table of mixed numeric and non-numeric data as a single array – in which, say, one column is of type numeric, another of type character string, and so on.

Data manipulation

Once we have described the data items to be processed, the language should allow us to state, in a meaningful and clear way, the operations that we wish to carry out on them. Where possible the means of expressing these manipulations should reflect the special terms of the problem area concerned. Thus, if the problems involve arithmetic, clearly the language must support arithmetic operations – using either symbolic notation (for scientists and engineers) or explicit notation (for people in commerce). We would like this for other types of manipulation, such as character handling, as well.

Once a language contains data description facilities which allow us to use more natural data structures within programs, the language should obviously let us work with (manipulate) such structures easily and safely. Ideally, it should let us assign structured data items to a single entity, without having to break down the assignment into component or atomic moves.

For instance, if an entry in a file is given as a row of array elements, it should be possible to assign a whole row of the array in a single operation. This makes programs easier to write, read and maintain. A further advantage of such a facility is that it allows a check at the time of program translation (compile time) that data of the correct type is involved. This would guard against the possibility of, for example, adding an employee's clock number to the age and assigning the answer to the number of children!

Of course, when we use structured data, it is essential to be able to access the components separately. This can involve reference to a particular array element – but is better by giving separate names to different levels or components of the data structure.

Data communication

All useful computer programs produce output of some kind; many require information which can be available only during the run. Thus, it is essential that a language include facilities for the input and output of data items. Ideally it should be possible to transfer entire data items without having to include special code for breaking them into and/or assembling them from atoms.

With the increased use of non-simple data types, there is more need to transfer information of a non-elementary nature. So, the language should support the transfer of entire record structures to and from files, with only a minimum amount of formatting information supplied by the programmer. In addition to the more obvious input and output transfers, the component structure of programs requires that data be easily and safely transferred between program segments or components.

Ideally, we should be able to use any data structure as a parameter between program components: preferably with the ability to restrict the mode of access from within a component (eg read only for input parameters, write only for output parameters). If a program component is to act as a function, it must be possible to return, as a result, any permissible data structure.

Sequence control

Computer programs which simply carry out a straight forward sequence of operations just once are seldom worth writing. So that we can more fully exploit the useful power of the computer, programs should offer suitable sequence control elements, such as repetition and selection. Ideally, the language should reflect the natural expression of these elements, such as IF ... THEN ... ELSE, REPEAT ... UNTIL, WHILE ..., FOR index = 1 TO max STEP x.

The availability of these features affects the way we design programs. Languages which do not offer such features may lead to badly designed programs if the program designer becomes used to thinking only in terms of the features available.

9.2 HOW LANGUAGES DIFFER

One major difference between languages is that, as we have seen, some are interpreted whilst others are compiled.

An interpreter starts with some sort of editor package, into which we can enter programs; it translates the instructions one by one at run time, carrying each out before translating the next. Thus no object code is maintained or even produced, and interpreted programs run much more slowly than compiled ones. Also programs can run only within the interpreter environment (eg to run a Basic program, you load the Basic interpreter first). As there are no program compilations, there are no error listings. Any branch or program segment not accessed during testing may have syntax errors which will show up only when the branch is first used.

Languages differ in the number and type of characters you can use for naming variables (labels), in the possible data types, and in the ranges of data items represented.

Also, the operators for the different types of data differ according to the application area; they generally resemble the natural way of expressing the operations involved (eg, ADD in COBOL and + in FORTRAN).

Input/output (I/O) facilities differ too. In some languages, for example, data has to go out a character at a time, while in others, we can formulate, format and transfer whole pages by one or two instructions. Printer control codes and selection of printer options are possible in certain languages.

The sequence control constructs of repetition and selection, if available, appear in many different ways. Depending on these, it may or may not be possible to have good program structure. Thus, the language may or may not support the construction of hierarchical or modular programs, with a natural separation of the components performing specific tasks. Some languages offer these in the shape of functions and sub-routines or sub-programs; COBOL has sections and paragraphs. Components may be separately compilable, which can greatly simplify development and testing. The depth of nesting of components usually has different limits in different languages, and recursion is not universally on offer.

Languages also differ in the types of data structure they can support. Most support at least a one-dimensional list or array in main store, while some have practically no limit on the number of dimensions. Arrays may also contain levels or group items to be processed together. COBOL gives one of the best structures for handling arrays – containing mixed types of variables and accessing them in different ways, even allowing a variable to be numeric at one time and non-numeric at another.

Some languages can operate on an entire array or linked list as a single operation while COBOL and others can transfer a record or an entire screen with a single verb: eg READ filename in COBOL, and INPUT field, field, field in Basic.

It may be possible to increase (or decrease) the space occupied by a program at run time. For instance, Pascal is a block-structured language in which storage space is dynamically allocated to each block as it is entered, and released automatically on exit. Also, a sort utility may create longer or shorter strings depending on the amount of space available. In some languages, unfortunately, this results in programs which suddenly start trying to "grab" more and more storage. The program is then unreliable, making its dynamism only a partial success.

A language is designed for an application. The closer it is to the terminology of the application area, the fewer the errors made, and the quicker the program development. Thus COBOL, being devised for commercial usage, naturally specialises in file handling and bulk data manipulation, uses explicit English-like statements, and offers a large number of facilities for formatting commercial reports. The compiler accepts terms like Debit and Credit.

In brief, a language becomes popular if it is easy for people from different disciplines to learn and use. Sometimes a slower language (like Basic) is more useful because it is general purpose, and can quickly be learned, and a program can rapidly be brought to a runnable state.

Very often a language becomes popular simply because it is used by more people. A large number of support programs and utilities become available, and it is easy to access the compiler or library programs. As a result, people may ignore a better language, because of the lack of familiarity or the lack of support routines.

9.3 ADDITIONAL FEATURES

To a greater or lesser degree, different programs can be strung together, and run – one within a second as a sub-program, or one after the other, called from a main program. The execution returns to the next statement after the CALL. We can achieve communication between these programs by sharing the variables placed in storage, ie by "passing variables".

Normally, a variable in a program is treated as local to the program within which it appears, the storage cell being released when the program ends. Variables can retain their values within a sub-program if they are passed to the new routine. In some languages, like COBOL and dBase, a variable may be declared as global; in that case it keeps its value and identity in all the various sub-programs and modes and can even be examined outside the program environment (which is useful in case of program failure).

"Chaining" of programs involves getting the operating software to start a new program on completion of the earlier one. The next program can often be an independent one, written in a second language and stored in executable code after compilation.

Indeed, many modern languages allow direct entry into a machine code (m/c) program which, on ending, hands control back to the high level calling program. Whenever required, we can provide a more efficient or a tricky segment in m/c, and overcome the limitations of the language in use.

Also, many languages have constructs and program structure which make it easy to generate independent modules.

Interactive terminals with monitors were introduced long after computers became generally used. Therefore, the early languages did not offer any facilities for screen handling – these were patched into the later versions. COBOL74, for example, allows you to define an entire screen for display by a single command. In comparison all the later languages were based on a screen-oriented philosophy, and fourth-generation languages handle all screen formats for the user.

As vast numbers of users from different fields started keeping their records on computers, languages became friendlier too – and started to offer high level facilities like file creation, file manipulation and report generation.

Compilers offer more or less ability to communicate with the operating software. Many later languages greatly reduce the need for the user to understand this.

In today's world the less restrictive a language, the greater its popularity. It is useful to be able to re-use data files under different packages and compilers. Many packages offer, at least, a utility to convert a data file generated in the package into a standard format, and vice versa.

Certain versions of Basic on micros also allow the direct control of input/output ports; this makes it possible to write a computer interface with special purpose devices in this language, eg in process control. This can also be done in Pascal and C. Thus inter-device communication becomes possible.

Again in micros, we can enter data directly into store, and view store contents by specifying the address.

Today, the aim of new languages is to eliminate the need for specialised programmers and to make the computer more truly the slave of the user – why not let it do most of the work of program development?

9.4   SOME COMMON PROGRAM LANGUAGES

Now we compare the languages COBOL, FORTRAN, Basic, Pascal and C and study their application areas, their strengths and their weaknesses. We also briefly examine the common properties of fourth generation languages, 4-GLs, such as dBase, Oracle and Sea-Change.

COBOL (the COmmon Business Oriented Language)

COBOL is file-oriented, and the commands are English-like "sentences" grouped into "paragraphs" placed in "sections" in "divisions". There are four divisions. All data is defined in the DATA DIVISION, which is thus separate from the code. Most machine-dependent areas are collected into an ENVIRONMENT DIVISION.

Meaningful labels and paragraph/section headers, along with explicit English sentences make the code comprehensible at a glance, and minimise the need for comments and documentation.

We can define complex data formats and manipulate them with grouping of items, mixing of different data types, and setting up of tables and arrays. This is also true for record and output formats.

COBOL is specially good with alphanumeric strings – they can be broken up or grouped together as desired, and inspected, replaced, compared and manipulated in a variety of ways. There are facilities for data validation during entry, such as class checks for determining the type of data character entered.

Three types of files may be created: indexed files (with automatic indexing being handled by the compiler), serial, and direct access files.

The program can handle errors of overflow and underflow and errors during file access, so that run time interruptions need not be dealt with by the user.

COBOL insists on a rather rigid program structure; it allows structured programming and independent modules and is specially good for separating data from code. It is not, however, ideally suited for developing a quick trial program and may be considered tedious by people who prefer symbols to English sentences.

COBOL is highly amenable to structured programming and has facilities for passing or sharing variables between sub-programs. It is possible to chain independently compiled programs after testing.

Although facing intense competition from other languages, COBOL has remained popular for a large number of years. This is partly because it is versatile and well suited to the application, and partly because of the large number of supporting utilities and library programs which have appeared over the years.

Every major change in computing requirements has seen a corresponding growth and standardisation in the language. New machines, including micros, have been equipped with COBOL compilers. As a result, it is one of the most portable languages, especially when the programmer sticks to the standard features of ANSI COBOL.

Figure 9.1 shows the COBOL language in action, with examples of data variables and the basic constructs. The value of COUNT is assigned to OUT-NUMBER. For calculation, there are commands like ADD, SUBTRACT, MULTIPLY and we can work out simple formulas using COMPUTE.

All I/O is done by READ and WRITE statements, while we can direct input and output to different devices without changing the program (by amending the ENVIRONMENT DIVISION). Screen/keyboard handling is, however, possible through ACCEPT and DISPLAY statements intended for low volume data transfers.

```
* Data variables:
Meaningful data names:
ANNUAL-INSURANCE-PREMIUM

Assignment:
MOVE COUNT TO OUT-NUMBER.
Calculation:
ADD 1 TO COUNT.
COMPUTE TAX = SALARY * 25 / 100.
I/O:
READ SALARIES-FILE
      AT END MOVE 'Y' TO EOF-FLAG.
WRITE MAIN-HEADING AFTER PAGE.
ACCEPT NUMBER-OF-ITEMS.
DISPLAY INSURANCE-SCREEN.
```

```
Sequence:
Free format, termination by fullstop
Selection:
IF . . . . ELSE   (fullstop)
e.g. IF SALES > TARGET
        WRITE SALES-LINE AFTER TWO
     ELSE
        SUBTRACT SALES FROM TARGET
                  GIVING DEFICIT
        DISPLAY DEFICIT-SCREEN.
     READ SALES-FILE.
```

```
Iteration:

PERFORM HOURLY-ANALYSIS 24 TIMES.
PERFORM FILE-PROCESS UNTIL END-FILE.
PERFORM MONTHLY-PROCESS
      VARYING MONTH FROM 1 BY 1
            UNTIL MONTH = 13.
```

Figure 9.1   COBOL constructs

The terminator of a sentence is a full stop, and we can alter the sequence of instructions by use of PERFORM and IF structures. In the example, one possible action is that two blank lines will be output to the printer (with two line feeds), and then the SALES-LINE (each printer line being treated as a record in a file) will be output. Alternatively, the DEFICIT may be worked out and displayed. Both branches end with the next record of the SALES-FILE being read.

Three iteration structures appear. HOURLY-ANALYSIS is a module which would be repeated 24 times. The set of statements constituting FILE-PROCESS repeat until one of the statements causes the setting of an end-of-file condition. MONTHLY-PROCESS would be repeated with the index (or integer variable) MONTH taking values from 1 to 12.

These constructs demonstrate the English-like nature of the language.

FORTRAN

FORTRAN, named for FORmula TRANslation, arose for scientific calculation. It is "compute-bound" rather than "I/O-bound" (which means that calculation rather than data transfer speed is the limit), so is very quick in working out complex formulas. The commands have a fairly fixed format and cannot be made very readable. There are many mathematical and scientific functions in the compiler, and FORTRAN can understand labels like *pi*.

Utilities for graph plotting and similar aids to numerical data analysis support FORTRAN. Reports produced through the language generally contain tables of numbers with minimal facilities for report and column headings or for labels. Similarly, it is not designed for locating particular items of data on large files. Its power is in handling numbers rather than character strings. Earlier versions had very limited character handling abilities, but these problems have disappeared with FORTRAN-77.

FORTRAN data variables are usually symbols, the labels being rather short. Statements can be numbered when necessary to be more easily identified. I/O commands indicate the device number (eg 2 or 4) and the number of a data format statement (eg, 31 or 32 here) to be used during the operation. The actual variables to be transferred are listed alongside.

A new line indicates a new command unless otherwise specified. Earlier versions of FORTRAN did not have sequence control structures to permit the development of structured programs and independent modules. This has been corrected in FORTRAN-77 with IF ... ELSE ... END IF. In the first example of Figure 9.6, control would branch to statement number 20 if A is less than 1.0, otherwise to number 30. In the next one, if AX is greater than 9 times AY, the value of X is assigned to T and AX is copied to X: otherwise both X and AX are set to 0. The DO statement requires that all following statements up to statement number 10 should be repeated with the index I taking all values between 1 to 6.

```
* Data variables:
Simple data names:
    X, I, NUM, AINT

Assignment:
A = 98.34
Calculation:
AREA = sinh (X) * EXP (1 -2 ** N)
Understands mathematical symbols
like 'e' or 'PI'
I/O:
READ (2, 31) X, AINT
WRITE (4,32) 'AINT =', AINT
```

```
Sequence:
    New line for each statement
    GOTO 20
Selection:
    IF <condn> <command>
    IF <condn> <branch numbers>
    IF . . . THEN . . . ELSE . . . ENDIF
e.g.   IF (A .LT. 1.0) 20, 30
        IF (AX .GT. 9 * AY) THEN
            T = X
            X = AX
        ELSE
            X = 0
            AX = *
        ENDIF
Iteration:
    DO 10 I = 1, 6
    :
    :
10 CONTINUE
```

Figure 9.2   FORTRAN constructs

The examples of Figure 9.2 should make it clear that the language is more suited to people who think in mathematical terms.

Basic

Basic was a language intended for beginners. It has some of the advantages of FORTRAN in being symbolic (therefore less wordy than COBOL) and in taking much less time to produce a working program. However, standards are not very rigorous and there are immense local variations (some able to offer huge structure and power). The standard language does not, of course, have the power of FORTRAN in scientific applications, but Basic is popular as its commands are easy to understand and use.

Most versions are oriented to on line interactive use. Basic can handle numeric as well as character data, arrays and files. It has a large number of functions, both numeric and for character handling. These facilities can be used to create many others, so Basic is adequate for most purposes.

As Basic has grown, it has proved to be invaluable, with features not available or not so easy to use in other languages. Many versions offer facilities for a direct interface with the hardware. Thus, it is possible in many versions to address and access storage cells and I/O ports and to enter data in binary, hexadecimal or octal formats. It also has many output control formats, including a graphics interface with the monitor and commands to directly set parameters like colour and brightness, sound pitch and volume.

All I/O commands, like those of FORTRAN, need to provide a list of the fields. Some facilities are provided for quick generation of columns in a report but you must think of each data item in each line, or each field in a record, whenever you want a read or write of any kind. Often formatting facilities are very limited, but there are enough defaults for the lay user.

Pascal and C

Pascal is a member of the ALGOL family of program languages, the name coming from ALGOrithmic Language. It was developed as a structured language to increase efficiency in use of procedures. A large program is broken up into independent blocks or procedures. Storage space is allocated dynamically when the block is entered and released on exit. All data items are local to the block and are lost, with the storage space, on exit. Thus, procedures can be written and tested and then put together within an overall structure.

ALGOL is important – though it never came into general usage, many languages which did are based on it.

Pascal is named after Blaise Pascal, the 17th century French mathematician and philosopher. It is versatile and handles both numeric and non-numeric data, as well as some additional data types, such as dates and pointers.

Pointers indicate the addresses of the storage cells of variables. These are useful for passing parameters between procedures when the parameter is required to return a changed value. For example, a pointer to the top of an array may pass from one block to a second, or a pointer to a parameter may pass to a function which operates on it and returns the new value.

Pascal also accommodates complex user-defined structures. It creates files in either binary or text format.

Pascal constructs automatically produce structured programs and greatly resemble the pseudocode we have been using. The code consists of procedures and functions which can be independently defined. It is often used in systems programming.

C is named after B, the language on which it is based. (An improved version of BCPL, Basic Computer Programming Language, was called simply B.) It is a step higher than assembly language, but you need a good insight into its working to be able to use it correctly. The language is full of symbols, operators and expressions, and is therefore even more notational than FORTRAN. C is block structured, consisting of many independent modules. Every high level activity (such as printer control) is written as a module and stored as a library routine. Any number of modules may be chained together in a program.

The heart of C is a small routine which is machine-dependent. All the rest consists of library routines built up and implemented in terms of the central portion. Depending on the availability of library routines, the compiler may or may not offer more facilities. The essential portion, however, is relatively very small.

It is easy to transfer C programs from one machine to another, as the minimum amount of compiler required is always very small. Most of C consists of library routines developed for different processing activities.

C offers byte by byte access to I/O and is very rich in operators, having several types. Being low level, it is more direct, and therefore much more efficient.

C is highly suitable for systems programming work. Many operating systems are written in C (starting with Unix itself). It is not very suitable for commercial applications – it can be tedious to write and not very easy to learn. However, because of its run time efficiency and the flexibility of a low level language, its popularity has been increasing, and it is often used in preference to any other high level language.

Study Figure 9.3 to see some Pascal constructs.

The assignment operator differs from the equality sign by having a colon before it. Languages developed later (such as Basic) are able to make this distinction from the context alone. Statements end with a semi-colon. A group of statements forming a procedure is enclosed between BEGIN and END.

Logical expressions are referred to by their other name of Booleans (after George Boole who first worked out their properties). Both IF ... THEN ... ELSE and CASE constructs are on offer for selection. All three loop constructs which have now become so popular were available in ALGOL-based languages, so appear in Pascal and C. Figure 9.4 shows something of this latter language.

Assignment, calculation;
count: = 0 ; count: = + 1;
I/O:
writeln ('sum of numbers =', sum);
readln (number);
Procedure:
begin
  :
end
Selection:
(i) if <Boolean expression>
    then <statements>
      else <statements>;
(ii) case <expression> of
        <value 1> : <statement 1>;
        <value 2> : <statement 2>;
        :
        <value n> : <statement n>;
    end;

Iteration:
(i)
for <control variable>:=
        <val1> to <val2> do
    <statement>;
(ii)
while <Boolean expression> do
    <statement>;
(iii)
    repeat
        <statement>;
    until <Boolean expression>;

Figure 9.3   Pascal constructs

In C, programs and modules are enclosed within brackets and named as shown. There are many commands for I/O, there being a sample here. "%d" is the format specification, which must appear explicitly in every input/output statement. The value of the variable is substituted at the point indicated, using an appropriate format.

```
Program structures:
main ()
    {
        :
        :
        :
    }
```
Assignment, calculation:
variable = expression;
I/O:
getf ("%d", data);
printf ("Sum = %d", sum);

Selection:
(i) If <expression>
        <statement 1>;
    else
        <statement 2>;
(ii) switch <expression>
        {
        case <value 1> : <statement 1>○
                        break;

        :
        case <value n> : <statement n>;
                        break;
        default : <statement>;
        }
(iii) <var> = <exp1> ? <exp2> : <exp3>;
        (pseudocode equivalent:
            if var = exp1
                then
                        var ← exp2;
                else
                        var ← exp3;
                endif;   )

Iteration:
(i) while <expression>   (The initial value is set
        <statement>;   to exp1; Incremented in
(ii) do   steps given by exp3;
        <statement>;   Statement executed
    while <expression>;   while exp2 is true)
(iii) for <exp1>; <exp2>; <exp3>
        <statement>;

Figure 9.4   C constructs

The CASE construct starts with a "switch", followed by the actual cases and the set of statements to be executed in each branch. BREAK signals the end of the branch.

Selection construct (iii) is one of C's special constructs. The value of either expression-2 or expression-3 goes into the variable, depending on the result of a comparison with expression-1.

9.5 SAMPLE CODE

I have coded a section of the program developed in Chapter 1 into different languages to show the variations in their features. Study the listings with care – how easy do you find the different languages to follow? How easily do they cope with the different needs of the specification?

```
PSEUDOCODE
      set countofnumbers to zero;
      set sumofnumbers to zero;
      read nextnumber;
      while not end-of-file
         do
           countofnumbers ← countofnumbers
                                      + 1;
           sumofnumbers ← sumofnumbers +
                                nextnumber;
         read nextnumber;
       endo;
      print countofnumbers;
      print sumofnumbers;
      if countofnumbers <> 0
         then
         mean ← sumofnumbers/countofnumbers;
         else
            mean ← zero;
      endif;
      print mean;
      close files;
      stop;
```

Figure 9.5   Program coded in PSEUDOCODE

```
COBOL:
    :
    MOVE ZERO TO SUM, COUNT.
    PERFORM READ-AND-COUNT UNTIL EOF.
    PERFORM FINALS.
    :

FINALS.
    IF COUNT-OF-NUMBERS IS NOT EQUAL
                        TO ZERO
        COMPUTE OUT-MEAN = SUM / COUNT
    ELSE
        MOVE ZERO TO OUT-MEAN.
    WRITE MEAN-RECORD.

READ-AND-COUNT.
    READ NUMBER-FILE
        AT END MOVE 'Y' TO EOF-FLAG.
    ADD 1 TO COUNT.
    ADD NEXT TO SUM.
```

Figure 9.6   Program coded in COBOL

```
FORTRAN:
    COUNT = 0
    SUM = 0
    WHILE .NOT. EOF (1)
      READ (1,4)
        COUNT = COUNT + 1
        SUM = SUM + NEXT
    WEND
    WRITE (2,5) COUNT
    WRITE (2,6) SUM
    IF COUNT # 0 THEN
        MEAN = SUM / COUNT
    ELSE
        MEAN = 0
    ENDIF
    WRITE (2,7) MEAN
```

Figure 9.7   Program coded in FORTRAN

```
    PASCAL:
begin
      sum := 0;
      count := 0;
      while note of(input) do
        begin
          readln(data);
          sum := sum + data;
          count:= count + 1;
        end;
      if (count <> 0) then
          mean := sum / count
      else
          mean := 0;
      writeln ('Total numbers entered =',
                          count);
      writeln ('sum of numbers =',sum);
      writeln ('mean =', mean);
end;
```

Figure 9.8   Program coded in PASCAL

```
    C:
main ()
    {
      :
      :
count = 0;
sum = 0;
while (getf("%d", &data != EOF)
      {
      count ++;
      sum += data;
      }
if (count != 0)
      mean = sum / count;
else
      mean = 0;
printf ("Total numbers entered = %d",
                          count);
printf ("sum = %d", sum);
printf ("mean = %f", mean);
}
```

Figure 9.9   Program coded in C

9.6 LANGUAGE STANDARDS

When attempting to compare the merits of the various languages, take care to ensure that the languages considered are properly defined in standards and that, if variations exist, the comparison either leaves them out or takes careful note of their local nature. For example, there are versions of Basic which distinguish between integer and floating point numbers, but this is by no means a standard feature.

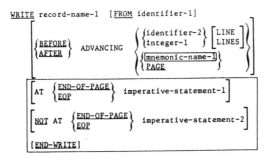

Sequential I-O - WRITE

4.7 THE WRITE STATEMENT

4.7.1 Function

The WRITE statement releases a logical record for an output file. It can also be used for vertical positioning of lines within a logical page.

4.7.2 General Format

WRITE record-name-1 [FROM identifier-1]

$$
\begin{bmatrix}
\begin{Bmatrix} \text{BEFORE} \\ \text{AFTER} \end{Bmatrix} \text{ ADVANCING} &
\begin{Bmatrix}
\begin{Bmatrix} \text{identifier-2} \\ \text{integer-1} \end{Bmatrix}
\begin{bmatrix} \text{LINE} \\ \text{LINES} \end{bmatrix} \\
\begin{Bmatrix} \text{mnemonic-name-1} \\ \text{PAGE} \end{Bmatrix}
\end{Bmatrix}
\end{bmatrix}
$$

$$
\left[\text{AT } \begin{Bmatrix} \text{END-OF-PAGE} \\ \text{EOP} \end{Bmatrix} \text{ imperative-statement-1} \right]
$$

$$
\left[\text{NOT AT } \begin{Bmatrix} \text{END-OF-PAGE} \\ \text{EOP} \end{Bmatrix} \text{ imperative-statement-2} \right]
$$

[END-WRITE]

4.7.3 Syntax Rules

(1) Record-name-1 and identifier-1 must not refer to the same storage area.

(2) Record-name-1 is the name of a logical record in the File Section of the Data Division and may be qualified.

(3) The ADVANCING mnemonic-name-1 phrase cannot be specified when writing a record to a file which is associated with a file description entry containing a LINAGE clause.

(4) Identifier-2 must reference an integer data item.

(5) Integer-1 may be positive or zero, but must not be negative.

(6) When mnemonic-name-1 is specified, the name is associated with a particular feature specified by the implementor. Mnemonic-name-1 is defined in the SPECIAL-NAMES paragraph of the Environment Division.

(7) The phrases ADVANCING PAGE and END-OF-PAGE must not both be specified in a single WRITE statement.

(8) If the END-OF-PAGE phrase is specified, the LINAGE clause must be specified in the file description entry for the associated file.

(9) The words END-OF-PAGE and EOP are equivalent.

Figure 9.10 Example page from a language standard

Each language standard is revised, re-affirmed or abandoned every ten years by an international body called ISO (International Standards Organisation); this has links with the world's national bodies, such as ANSI in the United States. Each language standard is developed by a committee and frozen in the form of a book, or manual: Figure 9.10.

A language manual adopts certain conventions when it presents the rules of the syntax of the given language. (These are generally explained at the beginning of the manual.) It is necessary to specify a way to represent the words involved.

Data consists of constants and variables (with labels, or identifiers). Combinations of these with operators form expressions.

Some words have to be reproduced exactly as they are, with the same spelling. These are the key (reserved) words; normally you cannot use them as, or sometimes even in, labels.

Each instruction involves some key words which are essential plus some optional ones which offer additional facilities.

There are also "substitution areas" in which the programmer must make appropriate entries. Often there is a set of options, of which you choose one, but not more than one.

Punctuation marks may be essential or optional. Items which may be used more than once in a statement (sometimes forming a list) are usually shown enclosed in some kind of curly or square brackets.

Statements in a language manual generally come in one of two categories: the declarative statements, such as those indicating data types and ranges, and executable statements, which form the body of the procedure.

Closely allied to the standard itself is the system of compiler validation. Using the standard as their source, various internationally accredited groups have developed independent tests to ascertain whether compilers conform to the various language standards. The United States government will not use any compiler that has not been tested in this way, having realised the benefits that conforming brings in terms of portability.

9.7 THE MYTH OF THE UNIVERSAL LANGUAGE

Since one of the stated aims of programmers is to communicate their ideas to others, including machines, you may wonder why there is not just a single Universal Program Language. It is obvious that such a language would vastly simplify the problems of systems implementation, machine replacement, software exchange and so on. And yet, after 30 years of commercial data processing, we are still a long way from this ideal.

There are many reasons for this: inertia, isolationism, vested commercial interest, inability to accept other people's ideas, etc. Within the commercial and scientific worlds of computing, the nearest we have come to this ideal is COBOL on the one hand and FORTRAN on the other. There is a growing use of various derivatives of Basic in both areas, whilst Pascal and Ada have yet to achieve universal acceptance.

It would appear that there is no simple solution to the multiplicity of program languages, since each performs tasks differently from the others, or performs tasks that the others cannot. The commercial world is currently suffering from a lack of programmers, so methods for developing programs more quickly have appeared; these are the fourth generation languages (or 4GLs) discussed in the next chapter. However, despite the fact that these languages have been developed entirely within the last few years, they have their own sets of problems and have not provided universal solutions either.

9.8   OPERATING SOFTWARE

The operating system is a major component of any large computer system. Except for the very smallest of machines, it is impossible to use a computer without one. An inefficient system can have an alarming effect on the throughput of a machine, often going so far as to completely nullify the effects of costly and fast hardware. Also, since it provides the only interface between the computer and the user, any deficiencies in the design of the operating software are a constant problem for the programmer.

An operating system is

> software which controls the execution of computer programs and which may provide scheduling, debugging, input/output control, accounting, compilation, storage assignment, data management and related services (USASI definition)

A simpler definition is

> a set of programs which permit the continuous operation of a computer system, from program to program, with the minimum of operator intervention

Before we look at the parts of a typical operating system, it is helpful to review the development of some aspects of computer operation.

The earliest computer systems had to be run manually by an operator, with the help of standard utility programs called exec (executive) programs.

The computer would read serial numbers identifying magnetic tapes and decide whether a particular tape was blank by looking for a header label, but it could not identify files on a tape. Therefore, each tape contained only one file. If the file were long, it spread to two or more tapes, but, if the file were short, the rest of the tape was wasted. A trailer label on each tape indicated the end-of-file or file-continued-on-new-tape status.

Only one program could reside in the system at one time. Thus, the operators had to be careful to sequence loading correctly, making sure all essential housekeeping tasks were complete before a particular program was fed in. They had to ensure that the correct data tapes were on line when required, and woe to a job if the paper labels on a tape were damaged or misread in any way!

Input/output peripherals, with their mechanical moving parts, can never match the speed of the entirely electronic processor; in earlier systems, this problem was even more acute than it is today. Output to a slow peripheral made the computer unavailable until the task was over. Sometimes, one or more work shifts of a computer could be reserved entirely for a particular printing job, such as a payroll. This added more time to system throughput (time between inputting a job and obtaining the output). The effect of lost time in this way increased as processors improved, increasing the disparity.

Thus, it is clear that before a program could be run, an operator first had to prepare for the job, load it, locate and load data files, and allocate peripherals. During the run, program events needed to be monitored with appropriate action being taken when requested. For handling different hardware elements, especially peripherals, several hardware control operations needed to be performed. Depending on the options required, switches needed to be set up in software interface registers.

The run had to be supervised, to ascertain that no error situation was produced – for example, with the computer locked in an infinite loop, or a missing CLOSE file command causing an invalid condition on the tape drive.

Occurrence of such error situations further aggravated the problems that already existed with manual operation. An operator had to take dumps of store contents, and collect diagnostic information – for example, by noting the contents of registers and the exact point at which the error occurred. He would then take steps to remove the error situation and load the next program.

The whole process had to be repeated for the next program. Scheduling of resources, handling program queues, and determining priorities were part of an operator's routine tasks, with accounting information being noted as required.

The action of the computer was thus largely dependent on service from a slow person, who had to be a specialist to be able to operate the machine efficiently. Far from being the servant of people, the machine required so much attention that often it was the other way round! The processor itself was idle for a large proportion of the time.

Systems became more efficient as hardware and software solutions were found. Hardware improvements produced more and more independent peripherals. They could handle transfer of complete records with minimal processor intervention and set a "ready" flag – or provide an interrupt signal – to state that the transfer was complete. The processor would continue with the next job until interrupted, or process the next job while scanning the flag at regular intervals.

Making off-line the input or output process became possible when special devices were produced to handle data transfer. The computer itself never handled the slow devices but used "images" of the contents of backing store. Software was then fed into the computer to handle such images, and the concept of a "supervisor program" began to emerge. Incoming data was not taken literally, but was interpreted (and appropriately formatted) by the supervisor program.

The routines for file handling were improved so that more than one could be written on one tape and the supervisor program could identify the required file. This not only made a more efficient use of magnetic tape space but also reduced operator intervention.

Standard routines dealing with file handling were combined with suitable operator messages, which were file based and could therefore be much more readable. This system was enhanced to handle simple batched (grouped) queues. Series of jobs were entered onto magnetic tape on a batch processing system, and the supervisor program automatically processed one job after another.

These supervisory programs eventually evolved into today's sophisticated operating systems.

The operating system (OS) provides the link between the user and the hardware. A program can be handed over to operating software (OS), which will then look after its needs and resume control whenever the program relinquishes it.

Allocation of hardware elements is completely handled by the OS. Whenever there is any battle for resources, the OS decides priorities and automatically queues the jobs in question.

As programmers and operators manage the computer through the operating system, facilities are provided by the system to make communication easier. The details of the requested task, such as the copying of a file, are also handled by the operating system. In addition to managing the machine, the operating system provides many facilities. It can keep an account of the use of different facilities by computer users. In commercial computer installations, it handles the budgets of the users and sends the bills to them.

Debugging aids are provided for the development of programs. We have already seen examples of this.

All data is managed by the operating system, from both storage and backing store devices. For example, a request for a data file access is handed over by a program to the operating system. The details of the file access are then managed by the OS. The OS thus relieves the programmer of routine hardware tasks. The program may contain minimal instructions on what is expected from hardware. Lastly, most operating systems on large computer systems take automatic back-up copies to ensure data security.

The next dramatic improvement in the capabilities of the computer came with the introduction of operating systems which allowed multiprogramming.

9.9 MULTIPROGRAMMING

Though work was speeded up by having the processor itself handle routine tasks through a set of operator programs, there was still a tremendous amount of time in which the highly expensive CPU (processor) was idle, waiting for a peripheral transfer. The next step was to create a means by which the CPU could switch from one program to another whenever it was waiting for a transfer.

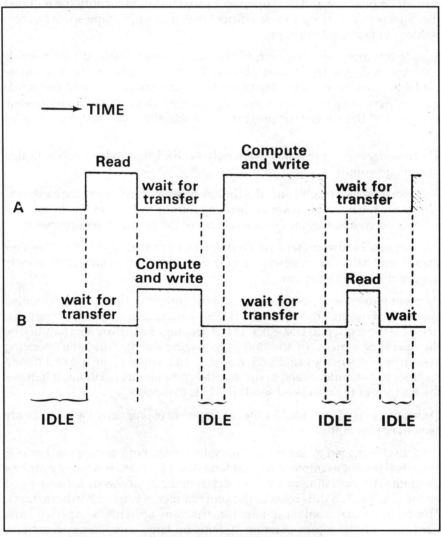

Figure 9.11 CPU utilisation in multiprogramming

The graphs in Figure 9.11 show CPU utilisation against time when it has initiated a transfer from a peripheral. Program A reads a file, makes some calculations and writes to an output file. For a large portion of the time, the CPU is idle waiting for the transfer to take place. I have exaggerated the graph – the CPU takes less time and waits much longer than shown.

In a multiprogramming computer, a second program, B, is in store at the same time. The supervisor detects when execution of A stops, immediately saves the values of the registers and flags, and hands over the CPU to the second program. When there is a pause in B (or when A is ready again), the current registers and flags would be stored in the B storage area, the values for A restored and control handed back to A. The exact details of the switch depend on the particular Operating System (OS). One of the earliest computers, the Leo III, could run 13 programs this way at once.

Storage for data as well as program instructions is allocated dynamically, and a priority system is used to determine which program should be serviced first, if more than one is ready for the CPU.

As mentioned, it is possible to switch off line the interface to a slow input/output device such as a printer. Outputs are queued (or spooled) onto backing storage media and passed separately to the printer to handle at its own speed. It is even possible to mix outputs to a spool, for different peripherals. The queueing of outputs to slow peripherals also makes it possible to continue processing when the peripheral is temporarily out of action, as the spool may be processed independently once the peripheral is back on the job.

The tasks of a multiprogramming supervisor are similar to those of a supervisor on a single program system, except that it handles more than one job and must keep track of each.

Programs load into independent storage areas. For each program, the system handles the input/output and backing storage files. This involves peripheral allocation, managing CPU time and priority control as we have seen already. Program activity is monitored for any program under execution. In addition a facility exists whereby a human operator can communicate with the computer and carry out job control tasks.

The more the OS has to do, the bigger it becomes and the longer it takes to do the work. Some operating systems in earlier versions occupied very large parts of the main store and the space available for users became severely cut. System throughput slowed so much as the OS began to take so long to decide what to do that even simple programs took a lot of time. Today's computer systems have very large amounts of store and much more efficient supervisor programs.

With the advent of on-line data entry terminals, the multiprogramming concept has extended to a situation where there can be several users accessing the computer from different terminals at the same time.

While multiprogramming takes place in a relatively controlled environment, multi-access working becomes completely uncontrolled. Each of the users access the CPU without any awareness of other users on the machine, and the OS shares resources between users in such a way as to maintain the illusion of each having sole control of the machine. A user should not be aware of operating problems due to the sharing of resources.

Techniques used could involve time-sharing, that is giving a fixed slice of time to each user, or there may be some other method of polling users to determine their requirements. Programs may be swapped in and out of memory, to offer more space. Comprehensive security and protection systems are necessary to safeguard the interests of every user.

With the development of techniques to increase the efficiency of end-user programs (for example in transaction processing), and with greatly improved hardware times for the CPU as well as peripherals, the multi-access machines of the early 1990s can offer simultaneous service to hundreds.

As multiprogramming systems require large amounts of store, some operating systems have developed the technique of using backing storage space as an extension of internal storage. Instead of swapping in an entire program, the program is handled in fixed page sizes and the operating system swaps in only a few pages of a program at a time: the current page and a few before and after it. The rest of each program always stays in backing store.

At any given time, the machine could be working with programs requiring more space than what is physically available. It is able to do this without degrading the system performance seriously. When used in this way it becomes a "virtual machine" – it seems to make available a store which does not really exist. It can also be made to mimic the existence of certain devices, such as a disk drive, which are not physically present.

The OS, however, becomes bigger, requiring even more store and power, and needs to be developed with care. At least one major virtual machine operating system had to be initially withdrawn because it actually reduced throughput rather than increasing it.

9.10 OS SUMMARY

The operating system on a modern machine has evolved from offering the least facilities into a form which is easy to communicate with and which handles most of the routine administrative jobs of the machine.

It includes the following features.

    a) *Command language:* a system language to cover the parameters required by the OS on input/output devices to be allotted, time limitations in or space requirements of a program, likely events and corresponding actions, and all the facilities offered by an operating system.

Commands may have keywords and/or parameter substitution areas. For example, the command STOCKVAL JANDATA REPOJAN indicates that the job to be run is STOCKVAL, and has an input data file JANDATA and an output data file REPOJAN. Usually, there is a facility whereby a string of commands can be invoked by a single command called a macro.

b) *Failure and recovery:* Any error situations, such as a peripheral failure or an attempted violation of storage, causes an interrupt to be signalled to the operator. The OS handles these by invoking error recovery routines which generally record enough data for failure diagnosis.

c) *File management:* Utilities are on offer for file creation, deletion and copying. For security, data files are grouped according to user and access classifications; they can be reached only through a hierarchy of levels with restrictions on access at each level.

d) *Logging:* Some sort of system journal is kept; in it the system records every occurrence, along with essential details and the time. This may be on backing store or as a console printout – output on a printer reserved for the system. In case of sudden failures, this gives valuable information regarding what was happening at the time: such as which jobs were actually in the system and may have been affected.

e) *Accounting:* Each use made of each facility is recorded with details of user and time. This information helps in billing or for working out wear and tear and for evaluating system usage, performance and areas in which expansion is required.

f) *Scheduling:* Determining priorities and servicing queues, taking decisions in cases of contention. This is done on the basis of priority ratings, urgency ratings or deadline inputs, according to which internal priority parameters are set and used during resource allocation. It must guard against loopholes such as to prevent a low priority job getting pushed down so often that it never runs. Sometimes human intervention is required, with manual override or a pre-scheduling by operators to give a good job mix.

g) *Operator communications:* These consist of essential messages to the operator such as signalling error situations, requests for loading of certain tapes or files, and notifying an end of job. They are generally kept to a minimum to avoid slow and error-prone (that is, human) activity and to make the computer more self-sufficient and independent.

h) *Security:* The multi-access facility makes it essential to restrict data access by users to safeguard their interests and prevent accidental or deliberate interference with files belonging to others. A system of passwords and access classifications is created and handled by the OS for this purpose.

The OS also generally provides a number of library programs and utilities as aids to programmers. System calls are requested by a program to obtain information regarding such parameters as date, time, space available on a disk, or information about a file.

Operating systems are developed for specific hardware. There may be a choice of OS, and the same OS could be changed to reflect other hardware configurations. The actual system used affects the way in which programs may be implemented, and often even the program design. The facilities on offer by systems differ widely − and may be easier or less so to use. It is, therefore, necessary to know the OS in use.

All access to the machine is through the operating system, and the user is therefore limited by its peculiarities and capabilities. The advantages of easy communication and the provision of a hardware interface far outweigh this disadvantage − except in some rare cases, mainly on micros, when a user may prefer to work without an OS.

In all business oriented applications, however, as with larger machines, security is essential and a user has to learn to work within the OS environment.

NOW TRY THESE . . .

Exercise One

What are the four essential features that a programming language needs?

Exercise Two

Two programs are in main store: the first is a main file update, whilst the second is a "type-to-print" program. Which program should be given priority by the operating system, and why?

10 Software utilities, models and tools

OBJECTIVES

When you have worked through this chapter, you should be able to:

- explain the nature of utilities and applications software
- give examples of utilities and applications packages
- outline the nature and use of program design tools, flowcharters, macros, pre-processsors, test data generators, and trace and snapshot systems
- describe some features of word processors of value to programmers
- outline the significance of spreadsheets and data base managers
- state what structured query language is, and how to use it
- outline how report generators and application program generators differ
- state the nature of fourth generation languages.

INTRODUCTION

In the last chapter we saw something of the development of software over recent decades. We leave you to think about the question "What will the future bring?" – but in our last chapter, we consider the alternatives to developing new programs.

It would be strange if, over those decades, a number of valuable applications programs had not appeared. Indeed they did – and many have very wide applicability to users' general and specific needs. A fast growing role for programmers, therefore, is to develop and amend those programs to meet the exact needs of their users.

Most programmers prefer to write their own programs for any application rather than having to modify existing routines for particular situations, or learning and adapting one of the proprietary packages that are available in ever increasing numbers.

In today's world, however, there are very many software aids which greatly simplify the programmer's work. New tools make the work of application development much less time consuming and are also removing much of the tedium associated with the development of a large and complex program. To some extent every programmer needs to keep up with new software releases and get acquainted with the facilities on offer.

10.1 UTILITIES AND PACKAGES

Operating software and language compilers, assemblers and interpreters are already familiar to programmers; they form a part of the software aids they use regularly. Other software aids belong to the categories of utilities and packages.

We need certain routines, for example, for sorting, in almost every application; they do not have to be written by every programmer. Such routines are available in a library of programs called utilities. These are written in a generalised way and may be adapted to a particular case by setting parameters.

Thus, a utility is a program (or set of programs) which may be incorporated into a software system to handle a particular task. It can be used only by someone who understands programming.

A package, on the other hand, is designed to handle an entire application, for example, a company's payroll. It deals with all aspects of the application. For example, in a business situation, it would generally consist of data entry and validation, some processing (involving, perhaps, calculations with numerical data or the collating of data), and the printing of reports. It gives messages prompting the user on what is required, and may therefore be run by a non-professional user also.

Any exceptional conditions which may arise are handled by the package itself, with an appropriate message being displayed. For example, if the disk space runs out during data entry, the package detects and handles the error condition, so that the user does not have to interpret and analyse error messages from the OS. Any organisation may buy a package off the shelf, or have a package developed to their own specifications.

General purpose application packages usually have defined parameters, set during installation. These adapt the system to the particular conditions required.

Many packages are very good − while others are not. There are, therefore, difficulties in evaluating a package before buying it. A particular package may not be adaptable to a firm's exact requirements − they may need to alter their manual system to fit the package. Special programs may be written to tailor the system, but, sometimes, this is not possible despite the availability of skilled staff. Unless the data is recorded in a convenient fashion, it is not always possible to produce special reports as required. In other words, some packages require considerable support, which may not be available locally.

However, the advantage to users is that they need not bear the development cost and can get the system at once. It is quite feasible for commercial users to buy their entire software in application packages, without needing to have a single program written.

10.2   FOR INSTANCE

The OS itself offers utilities for file maintenance and copying and for sorting and merging files. Housekeeping tasks, required to keep a large computer system in order, are also available as utility programs. Thus, there are utilities to copy files from disk to tape, for printing files held on backing store, for detecting and using erased regions of store and so on.

Packages are generated for use in a variety of applications – for example, in mathematics, engineering and in the business environment. Linear programming is a good example – it is an optimisation technique to find the best possible solution to a problem which requires an analysis of multiple parameters. For instance, in engineering, packages aid the design of mechanical structures and working out the stresses in different parts of the structure after loading them.

Comprehensive business oriented application packages are now also readily available. Some examples are: the control of stock moving in and out, the planning and scheduling of jobs or the loading of machines in the production room and, of course, computerised financial management. There are a large variety of accounting packages catering for different kinds of business.

10.3   DEVELOPMENT TOOLS

Design tools

Earlier in the book, I claimed that any program could be written using the basic logic structures of sequence, selection and iteration. We met the Jackson method of program design which related these structures to the input and output data to produce a program structure. Because of the simplicity and flexibility of these three constructs, they have proved to be the ideal vehicle for conversion to a graphics based design tool which gives each structure in symbol form. The program can be designed on screen using the same notation as a structure chart, but with checks for consistency added and enforced automatically. Most will produce pseudocode from the diagrams, and some will use this to generate a version of the program in a particular language such as COBOL or Ada.

The program is shown as a structure diagram on screen; any changes to the program simply involve making the appropriate changes to this chart. The programmer no longer deals directly with the code, and the programmer/program interface is at a higher level of abstraction. This has advantages in that the program is easier to follow in picture form, and is documented automatically, while some of the potential programming errors are removed. Against this there is the disadvantage that the source code produced is likely to be hard to follow and maintain below the design level.

Flowcharters

Flowcharts are steadily losing their popularity as a development aid. When they are used, they vary quite considerably from the eventual code. Flowcharters are programs which do the job in reverse and produce a flowchart from an input source code. Thus, they may (though not often) be useful in documenting programs and giving a pictorial representation.

The drawing may be produced on listing paper, sometimes showing just the outlines and leaving it to the programmer to fill in the details. Some use plotters to get better quality output.

Macros and macro-processors

A macro can extend the instruction set of a machine by defining a new instruction, consisting of a series of existing instructions. The macro is named, defined by specifying the list of instructions, and called by quoting its label. A macro-processor then substitutes the list in place of the name.

This facility was first provided by assemblers – as assembly level commands are very limited and need to be combined for most purposes.

```
Assembler level instructions
      10 X    (LOAD copy of X into accumulator)
      11 X    (ADD X to accumulator)
      12 X    (copy accumulator into X)

Add X to Y
      10 X    (bring in X)
      11 Y    (add Y to it)
      12 Y    (store result in Y)

$MACRO SUM P,Q
            10 P
            11 Q
            12 Q

$END M
      .
      .
      .
      .


  SUM X,Y
      .
      .
      .
      .
```

Figure 10.1   Macro example

The example in Figure 10.1 shows how an instruction to add X to Y may be shown in assembler. Operations may be carried out between one memory location and the "accumulator" (a special store in the processor) only. It shows three assembly level instructions. Each instruction consists of an operation code and an operand.

Thus, 10X tells the computer to copy the contents of X into the accumulator, while 12X would result in the converse. 11X would cause it to add the contents of X to the accumulator.

To add X to Y, the first number must be loaded into the accumulator, the second added to it, and the result transferred from the accumulator to Y. A macro called SUM may be defined which can add any two numbers, P and Q. The programmer can now use the command SUM, and substitute his operands in place of P and Q instead of defining the process each time. The macro-processor replaces the command with the defined set of three instructions, producing the addition.

Note that a macro differs from a sub-routine – there a CALL actually transfers control to a routine and returns it to the calling program at the end. Also, languages like Basic have a function definition facility similar to the above.

We can use general purpose macro-processors to translate macros into higher level languages such as COBOL and FORTRAN. For example, a COBOL pre-processor may be used to translate macros into COBOL. Programmers may define macros translating pseudocode constructs according to their own styles of programming. The coding of the pseudocode would then be handled by the macro-processor.

Data generators

These software utilities generate test data according to a specified format. See Figure 10.2.

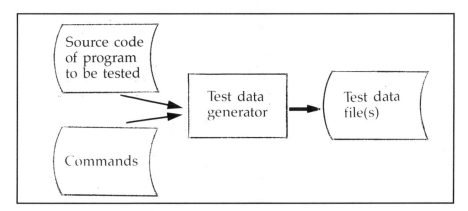

Figure 10.2   Test data generator

The program source code is fed in, along with the user commands. The generator examines the requirements and accordingly produces one or more data files. For example, it will use the data division of a COBOL source program to generate appropriate data. The package may give data of different types, as shown in Figure 10.3a, b, c.

A pseudo random number generator which can:

- produce random numbers evenly distributed over a specified range

- produce the common distribution is (eg Poisson, Normal)

- produce random numbers to any base (eg hex, binary)

- produce random bit patterns

- produce random numbers with given restrictions (eg all odd numbers, the 1, 4, 7, 10 ... (3n—2) set,

- produce any of the above repeatably, to enable comparative testing

---

Figure 10.3(a)   Test data generator features

An alphanumeric string generator which can:

- produce strings of alphanumeric characters of a fixed length or a variable length (eg between 5 and 7 characters)

- produce strings of fixed or variable length as above but with one or more characters fixed (eg always starting with Z9, or first character always numeric)

An error case generator which can:

- generate random or specified errors in the data (eg outside range or wrong type or incorrect format/picture)

- limit the number of random errors generated (none if required)

- ensure that all possible error combinations have been tested

---

Figure 10.3(b)

A file generator which can:

- generate files with fixed length records (with features as specified previously)

- generate files with variable length records (with or without specified limits)

- generate files which require more than one reel of tape, or disk or diskette (multiple-volume files)

- generate records with constant fields

- generate records with a sequence

- generate files in a specified sort sequence

Figure 10.3(c)

Note that some so-called random number generators, unless created through very elaborate devices, cannot produce truly random output – they are also pseudo-random number generators.

Trace and snapshot

Trace packages monitor programs during execution and produce reports (or "snapshots") of what is being done by the program and what the results are. The reports include more or less detail – right down to statement by statement reporting.

For a well designed and systematically developed program, such a package should not normally be necessary – unless you have very little ability to debug, or the program is very complex. Regular dependence on such a facility is really "scraping the barrel" as far as concerns skill in programming!

More recent developments have produced much more effective symbolic debuggers. Trace packages can be useful when working interactively – some of them allow you to interrupt program execution and modify variables by using their symbolic names (labels). This can cut down debugging time. Even this use, however, is like using a sledgehammer to crack a nut and is not to be encouraged as common practice.

10.4 APPLICATIONS SOFTWARE

Word processors

Every programmer needs a facility by which programs can be entered onto the machine before being compiled and run. Some form of line editor is generally offered by an OS; through it, you may enter lines of code into a file in text (ASCII or equivalent) format. The file may be retrieved later, and edited as required.

A word processor (WP) offers a far more elaborate facility for text storage, manipulation and retrieval. The display screen is part of a page of text. The cursor may be placed anywhere on the screen and you may add, delete or modify characters, words or even lines. In addition, there are several other facilities.

Text formatting lets you specify the length of a page, its margin, page headings and footings – the system automatically takes care of these as you enter the text. When a line becomes too long, the next word is moved to the next line until there is a paragraph break.

A block of data may be defined and operated on, eg, moved to a new place, deleted, or copied to within the same or a second file. Text may be inserted from another file.

A particular item of data may quickly be found in a large file by specifying a page number or group of words to be found by the processor. There are facilities for printing text to the specified format, with printer control instructions being introduced by the WP. It can handle special printer settings – such as character fonts (shapes) and sizes, highlighting, underlining, and printing characters as super- or sub-scripts.

WP packages may also aid file manipulation, ie copying, deleting or renaming files. A back up copy of the earlier version is often automatically produced when a file is edited.

Spreadsheets

Here, the display screen and computer store are divided into a set of cells organised into rows and columns. Each cell can store one data item. Data can consist of numbers or a set of words, but is most often used to store numerical data arranged and manipulated in columns, as, for example, in accounting.

Thus, the cursor may be moved up or down one cell at a time to choose a particular row and column and enter, delete or edit data. It is possible to set relations between columns or rows, and to define processing operations for an entire column.

Most spreadsheets include graph commands, which let you view the whole or a part graphically. Printouts may be obtained of the spreadsheet and the summaries and graphs.

In addition, it is quite common now to see "integrated" packages containing a spreadsheet, a database, a word processor and a time-management facility all in one. Data is passed between the component programs quite easily by means of a "clipboard", which is a common data area available to all parts of the package.

Data bases

In any organisation, different views of the same data are required by the different departments. As each department creates files for its own use, multiple copies of the data are produced.

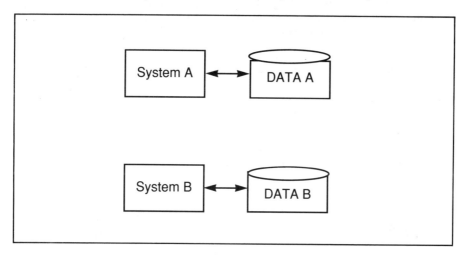

Figure 10.4 Multiple Data Files

When one department, for example, the sales department, updates its data files, the remaining data becomes out of date until the other departments receive their notifications and update their own files. Output reports would therefore depend on the file used during processing.

If a department wishes to change its software system to enhance or update the facilities, the data files often need changing too. The converse is also true: any change in the organisation of data, introduced, perhaps, to improve access time, would mean that all the programs must be changed.

Data becomes unified and independent of program with the introduction of a central (shared) data facility. Data required in an installation is stored in a set of "data base" files; all users may access these, according to their security classifications. The data base is maintained and accessed with the help of a software system known as a data base management system or DBMS.

The DBMS consists of two parts: a Data Description Language (DDL) and a Data Manipulation Language (DML). The DDL is used to specify the data which is to be included in the data base; the DML is used to access the data. The DBMS will provide file handling facilities and will also allow the actual data to be held separately from the programs. Thus programmers do not have to be concerned with the size of data items, or the way in which data is structured, all that they need do is specify the fields required and the DMS will obtain them. In terms of program maintenance this means that if a field changes its size or content then only those programs that use the field directly need to be changed. This is much easier than conventional fields where every program that accessed the file containing the changed field has to be checked and possibly amended. The advantages of using a DMBS purely as a mechanism for obtaining and controlling access to data are sometimes sufficient for an organisation to adopt it, and to go no further towards implementing a true data base.

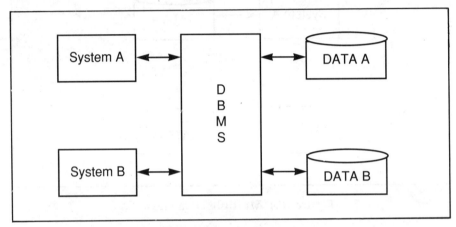

Figure 10.5 A DBMS

A real data base approach requires a more comprehensive approach to the concepts of data and information. In a conventional file-based system each application is developed independently using its own set of data. This results in large area of duplication of data, and extra work keeping the information up-to-date. A true data base approach requires that an organisation's data is considered as a whole and that the data structure is designed to reflect this. Any duplication of data is minimised and controlled.

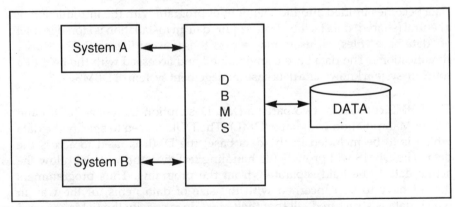

Figure 10.6 A Database System

The ideal is that each data item is only entered once and is then available to all users of the system. This approach firstly reduces the amount of storage needed for data, and secondly reduces the inconsistencies that could arise from the same information being held in more than one place.

There are several types of database structures: relational, hierarchical and network, the most popular of which is the relational database. The relational model is based on a collection of data in tabular form. This structure is similar to a series of simple sequential files (call 'relations') within which exist records (called 'tuples'). This can lead to some confusion between relational databases and systems that should strictly be called 'file-management' systems. Typically these allow the user to set up and maintain a small number of files, sort, retrieve, data, and output, rather like an electronic filing cabinet. Relational databases on the other hand are groups of tables related via repeated fields so that a record in one table can link to a corresponding record in another.

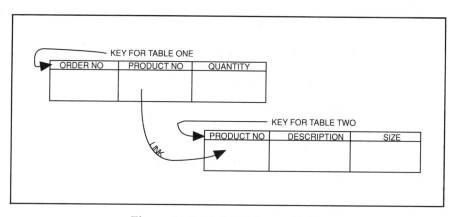

Figure 10.7 Links Between Tables

You have probably noticed that this structure causes records in different tables to contain repeated fields; for example 'product no' has to appear in both table one and two to create the link. This is the only time that duplication (or 'redundancy') of data is allowed.

Data is accessed through a query language, the statements of which can be used either directly from a terminal, or embedded in another programming language like COBOL. The best known query language is Structured Query Language (SQL) which is an internationally recognised standard and has been adopted by many manufacturers of database systems. The basic set of SQL commands consists of CREATE, SELECT, INSERT, UPDATE and DELETE for updating the tables and obtaining data.

Creating a table using SQL would require the following statement:

```
CREATE TABLE      tablename
       Keyfield     type     conditions, other fields     type
```

To differentiate the keyfield in this example, it would have "UNIQUE" as one of the conditions. Once created, the records in a table would be updated as follows:

```
UPDATE tablename
SET
     fieldname = fieldname Change
WHERE
     keyfield = value of key required
```

or new rows inserted by:

```
INSERT INTO tablename
              (fieldnames with values)
VALUES (values to be inserted)
```

Rows can be deleted as follows:

```
DELETE
FROM tablename
WHERE
     keyfield = value to be selected
```

These relatively simple examples can only serve as an introduction to SQL since it is complicated enough to warrant whole books on its own. Further features include the ability to update several tables using a single statement, and to retrieve data from several different tables by the simple use of individual SELECT statements.

SQL may be used in an interactive on-line mode or as a batch in a program. As a decision support tool, it results in the development of structured code, making it relatively easy to develop error-free programs.

With today's networked computers, the availability of a central data base facility makes it possible to use data files at widely different physical locations as a part of a single data base.

Report generators

A large part of commercial data processing activity consists of file maintenance, data retrieval and report generation. A report generator is a software utility which has been specifically designed to enable these tasks to be programmed easily and rapidly.

The most common form of report generator is effectively a high level language translator; it accepts as input a program (command sequence) written in a highly problem-oriented language, and generates a machine language program from it. The input language is easy to learn and, because of the formal and restricted nature of the commands, it is not hard to ensure that the logic is correct.

Report generators are mainly aimed at producing printed reports from files in backing store. In addition, many of the functions expected of a commercial language (such as COBOL) may be performed: for example, maintaining files, performing calculations, looking up tables, and branching to library sub-routines in other languages.

The specifications needed to define the problem and control the generator are drawn up on standard forms, ready for input to the computer. The parameters will define such things as these.

File description	–	specifying file names, input and output devices associated with these files, record sizes, block lengths, etc
Input	–	a description of record layout of input files, identifying the records by name
Output	–	a description (or picture) of the layout of records on output files, controlling the timing of their output by means of control breaks
Calculation	–	specifying the operations on the input data, and on intermediate data produced from other calculations

By far the best way to describe the contents of a report file is by means of a decision table. FILETAB enables a decision table to be used directly as input, thus reducing the chances of error by further simplifying the procedure.

Report generators provide a concise system, whereby non-technical staff and management can answer simple enquiries involving retrieval and report generation. Using such a generator, data processing staff may simply and quickly carry out quite complex tasks associated with reporting, enquiries, updating and the creation of files. Although a report generator is not as comprehensive as, say, COBOL, it can save considerable programming effort in many data processing applications; firms report increases in productivity of up to 80% after changing to FILETAB.

4GLs

Fourth generation languages (4GLs) are designed to be user friendly and interactive, and to help you quickly develop an application package.

Most data processing activities consist of data input and validation, file update, file querying and report production. 4GLs handle these activities, often through a set of menu driven screens which let you quickly choose what you want. Thus, there are menus for input definition, data definition and update, for procedure definition, and for report definition.

Any commands required are usually in a non-procedural form – in other words, the activity and file definitions are specified by the user, and the corresponding code to accomplish the activity comes from a "command processor", an integral part of the 4GL.

The organisation of data into traditional files has given way to the data base concept; here data is maintained as a central facility, to be shared by all users within the organisation. It is designed for much more efficient access.

Commands are at a very high level: for example, entire reports may be constructed and printed by a single command. File viewing (simple data queries), editing and indexing are simple matters, all intermediate steps being taken care of automatically. Data may be viewed logically by fields, the actual physical organisation and sequence of fields being no concern of the programmer.

Default assumptions are intelligent: often there is no need to specify all parameters.

For most requirements, a user need not be an expert nor be able to write programs. Programs are generally interpreted, with a word processing package provided, but may be compiled after testing. There are many debugging aids.

Application program generators (APGs)

One type of 4GL is an application generator package. This usually offers the facilities required in a normal data processing (DP) job, ie for input definition, data definition, procedure definition, and report enquiry definition. The code corresponding to the definition is automatically generated.

During input definition, the formats and linking of screens for data input and the data validation procedures may be specified by displaying the requirements on the screen. The types, ranges and other details of the data may be defined by filling out a form presented by the package. Procedures may be defined through the use of very high level commands, or by answering a questionnaire.

Commands may be used to set a view of data for report generation, and report formats may be specified by filling out forms. Sample formats are drawn for defining requirements, and outputs may be readily obtained when an APG is used. Therefore, a prototype can be presented to and verified by the user, before the entire package is developed. More user involvement is possible at every user stage and, in a routine application, it may not be necessary to do any programming at all.

Application packages

An application package is a program (or set of programs) specifically designed for use in more than one environment or organisation. Applications packages exist for all the common computer applications. For some of the most popular machine systems, a user need not write a single program in order to run an effective installation. The routine accounting and basic data processing applications are in the main covered by packages supplied by bureaux, software houses and consultants. Some more complex applications have been provided by computer manufacturers. You may gain some idea of the coverage offered by packages from the following list. (There are plenty more!)

Production control	–	production scheduling
		bill-of-material processing
		parts explosion and listing
		workshop loading
		cost centre performance
		labour costing
Stock control and inventory management	–	forecasting
		automatic stock replenishment
		costing
		purchase order preparation
Payroll	–	piece work calculations
		bonus calculations
		"gross to net"
		tax calculations
		year end tax accounting

Accounting and costing	– –	sales ledger sales analysis credit control purchase ledger nominal ledger standard and job costing
Mathematical	–	linear programming vehicle scheduling depot siting
Engineering	–	highway design "cut and fill" vehicle design circuit design frame loading and analysis
Miscellaneous	–	share registration mailing lists critical path analysis discounted cash flow word processing

The quality of available packages varies greatly. Many are thoroughly tested, very well documented and highly adaptable. As such they offer users a flexible and immediately available solution to information processing problems. Unfortunately, there are also plenty of packages which can be used only if the users adapt and distort the problem to suit. Such packages should be avoided; though detecting them can pose quite a problem.

A particular point to bear in mind when choosing a package is its support and/or ability to adapt to essential changes in the problem parameters. There are still payroll packages around which have to be rewritten whenever there is a change in the basic rate of tax.

Users and potential users should remember that applications packages are no substitute for trained, experienced staff. All too often, the major cause of disappointment and failure to achieve the full potential of a particular package is the lack of a proper understanding of the problem and the techniques involved in its solution.

became clear that in-house analysis and programming were a much cheaper and effective means of software production. Unfortunately expertise was rare and the demand for skilled IT staff far exceeded the supply.

The desire to obtain competent analysts and programmers stimulated the interest in defining the contents of these jobs in a way that could then be taught, and in turn analysed, to produce more efficient development methods and tools. The catalysts in this process were the users; after all it was they who paid the bill at the end. Indeed it was their exasperation at getting systems that were often over-budget, over-time and not to specification that forced the change in culture that was necessary for a scientific approach to software development to be adopted.

10.5 THE PROJECT TEAM

Introduction

Software development has changed a lot since the days when systems were designed 'on the back of a cigarette packet', sometimes literally! At that time systems analysis and programming were considered to be 'crafts', and as such not suitable for any kind of scientific definition. This meant that for many years the mechanics of analysis, design and programming were shrouded in mystery. During this period many organisations realised that computerisation meant increased efficiency and productivity and began to introduce computers on a large scale. Initially this was achieved by using the skills of external systems analysts and programmers, but it quickly

Systems analyst

When a new system is being developed the bulk of the initial technical work is done by systems analysts. The technical role of the analyst is described fully in Chapter 8, but briefly it comprises:

a) the provision of information about the feasibility of computerising existing systems;
b) the analysis of existing systems;
c) the design of the computer system that will supplement or replace the existing system.

The programmer

The actual implementation of the design will be done by a group of programmers. The programmer's role is:

a) checking the program logic in the design;
b) coding and testing the programs;
c) developing documentation relating to the programs.

The Quality Assurance Team

The quality assurance team has the job of developing quality standards for systems development, and enforcing the standards agreed for the project.

The Operations Department

Although not directly connected with developing a system, the operations staff play an important part in a peripheral way, by providing advice relating to network or database usage of the organisation during the project planning phase, and technical support to users during systems implementation and afterwards.

NOW TRY THIS...

Exercise One

If you were specifying the contents of a programmer workbench tool, what kind of features would you want, and why?

Appendix 1

Glossary

algorithm

set of precise steps that can solve a given problem, or a proof that the problem has no solution. In IT people express algorithms in various ways:

- in clear English sentence
- in pseudocode, somewhat like program code (and, indeed, a program is an algorithm itself)
- as a structure chart
- as a flow chart.

The solutions of all but the most simple problems involve branching – making a decision and then taking one of two or more paths. The decisions are of two types – conditionals and loops.

alpha-numeric data

data items that may contain letters and digits; indeed, to most people now, string data, whose items can consist of any set of keyboard characters array data structure, available in most program languages, for storing a fixed length list (one-dimensional array) or table (two- or multi-dimensional array) of items.

ASCII

the American Standard Code for Information Interchange, a world-wide standard for the storage and transfer of characters.

assignment

giving a value to a label (variable). The assignment instructions that do this have various forms. The simplest is like LET vat-rate = 15 (though many program languages don't use the LET keyword, and ":=", for instance, may replace "="). In an interactive program, the input instruction also includes assignment; non-interactive software may READ from DATA statements instead to give the same effect.

215

batch set of programs or program tasks passed to a computer for batch processing, action without people being involved. Most computing jobs are designed for batching, in order to trouble users as little as possible. Batch processing is the main mode of operation of main frame systems; the operating software includes a job control language (jcl) for the purpose.

binary chop
(or binary search) a very efficient way to search a list (for instance) for a particular value, as long as the list's search field contents are in order. It involves looping through this process until the search succeeds or it's clear the target isn't in the list:

> move to the item at or next below the centre of the list
>
> IF the target's less than that item, discard the second half of the list
>
> OTHERWISE, discard the first half.

block chunk of a program that handles a clear separate task and, indeed, may stand on its own or be stored in a library of procedures. Many program languages have a block structure: they expect programs to be developed and set out in blocks.

branch point in a program where the system will choose between two or more actions.

bug error in a program that means the program doesn't work as it should, de-bugging being the process of finding and squashing bugs.

code computer program, usually in a machine or assembly language, coding being the same as programming.

compiler software that translates a high level language program into machine code so the system can then run it. Compilation is the process of translating, with compilation errors being those that then come to light.

condition expression whose value is either true of false. On the basis of the value the system can then "decide" what to do at a branch point.

constant data item that's fixed in value (eg the firm's name, or PI, 3.14159...) throughout a program.

data set of one or more items of information inside an IT system, ie while being stored, processed or transferred. The word has changed from plural to singular in recent years; instead of datum, we now use data item to mean the singular (a unit of data).

Data control involves checking that the data that enters and leaves an IT system is in the correct form. The people concerned may use a data dictionary to show all the necessary details. This is a full statement of a system's use of data – for each data item and label: the meaning, relationship with others, form, type and usage. The purpose is to ensure system efficiency and to help with changes.

Data structures are different logical ways of viewing sets of data; each has advantages for processing in different contexts. A single data item is the simplest data structure – it may be an integer, a real number, a character string, or a Boolean (item with only two possible values) – these being different data types. We can picture a data item as a zero-dimensional data structure (like a mathematical point). Other structures involve more dimensions.

debugging process of removing (squashing) bugs in a program or hardware unit. The hardest part of debugging is finding the problems in the first place – tests need careful design so they cover as many situations as possible.

decision table in program documentation, a table listing all labels (variables) in the program with their meanings, and with notes on what should happen if they hold certain values.

declaration statement at the start of a program (eg in Pascal and some assemblers) that defines a label with its data type, or some other data structure with its size and type. That is a global declaration; a local declaration does the same at the start of a procedure, and applies only within that procedure.

desk check working through the listing of a program as if one is a computer: in order to try to find logical and other errors.

diagnostic

suitable for understanding the cause of (ie diagnosing) errors. Diagnostic aids for programmers include breakpoints, tracing, input testing systems, and diagnostic messages (error reports), all provided perhaps by a diagnostic program in the program language software.

dialect

non-standard version of a program language. Basic suffers more than most from dialects (there being hundreds in this case). The problem is that a program written in one dialect for one machine won't transfer easily to a different computer. On the other hand, allowing dialects allows fast development – so Basic has now become much more powerful than most other program languages.

documentation

the set of user instructions, background information, and notes on possible further development that (should) come with a hardware system or software package. As storage costs fall, it's more and more common to find most of the documentation on disk rather than in print. Most system designers and programmers don't write well, and/or don't think documentation important. As a result this material, though crucial, is often skimped or written by someone without full knowledge of the product.

dry run

working through a program "by hand" but as a computer would, in order to seek errors – an important part of program development and testing.

element

N 1 member of a set of similar items. An element of a data structure (such as an array) is one of its data items, though in a few program languages an element is a single data item that is NOT part of a structure.

environment

set of hardware and software needed by a program.

execution

carrying out (running) a command or program (set of instructions). An execution error is the same as a run-time error: an error in coding a program that shows only when the system runs the program.

expression

string of labels, constants and symbols that has a single value a program can work out (though the value may change from moment to moment). For instance, 2*PI*radius is an expression.

external sort sort algorithm working on a file held in backing store rather than in main store.

field space for one item (or in certain cases, block) of data. In a data base or file, a field is the space within the record of an entity (person or thing) for one attribute (characteristic) of that entity – eg part number, gender, half life. If the field is the basis for a search of a file, we call it a key field; in any event, all fields in a data base have field names (labels) by which we can refer to them.

Field testing is having people run a new program in real conditions (maybe as a pilot or parallel system) in order to find out problems.

file perhaps the most important data structure, one we can view as an array whose fields don't have to be the same data type or size. More generally, a file is any adequately organised set of data in an IT system (main store or backing store) – so people talk of program files as well as data and picture files.

flag indicator of some special situation or condition, sometimes called marker, pointer, sentinel, tag.

flow chart method of showing an algorithm or process (or a structure) in block form. The shapes of the blocks show the nature of each action or part, there being several standards that apply.

In IT, flow charts are common for showing the processes involved in a program (also, of course an algorithm) – but see structure chart; a system flow chart, as used by a systems analyst or designer, shows the events within a whole information handling system.

format overall shape or layout. Thus the format of a page of text includes such matters as the size of the four margins and of the gutter between any columns, the style of justification, the use of headers and footers, the style of headings and sub-headings and the use of block highlights (eg boxes).

global comprehensive, able to apply to a large range of cases or objects if not a complete set. In a program, you may call a global function from, and use a global variable in, any part of the program – rather than just (locally) within one procedure.

hierarchy　　relationship between objects (or people) which involves different clear levels of importance. It's normal to have the most important level at the top. Hierarchies tend to be like a pyramid in shape (think of the staffing of a large computing department). However, as they also tend to involve branching from level to lower level, we mostly view them as trees (like family trees). Indeed the data structure called a tree is exactly like this. A data base is a tree-like hierarchy too – with, in the lower levels, files, records and fields.

A hierarchy chart is a structure chart, a tree-like block diagram of all or part of a program as used in program development and documentation.

high level
program language　　program language in which each instruction translates to more than one machine code instruction. The higher the level of a program language, the more straight forward people find it to work with – but, on the other hand, the less able it is to use the specific features of the hardware, and the more complex is the translation process.

identifier　　name or label of a data item, program block, or instruction, as defined in a program for instance.

indent　　format a block of program so its left margin differs from the norm. This helps the reader see the program structure clearly.

index　　alternative name for the subscript of a data item in a data set (eg array). If the data set has the name sample, the items are sample(1), sample(2), sample(3) ... sample(n); here the value in brackets is the item's index (or subscript) – if a store holds the data set, the index of each item quickly leads the system to it.

information　　that which adds to human knowledge, ie which has meaning. In an information technology (see IT) system (when during transfer, under process, or in store) the coded representation of information has no meaning as such; we then call it data. Thus information becomes data when it enters an IT system; at the output side, it becomes information again when a person has access to it. People widely use data and information as the same, however.

input　　process of getting data from outside into the store of an IT system, perhaps for processing and for later access. It needs some kind of peripheral hardware, an input unit. This either can access data automatically (machine readable input) or needs a person to do the work.

integer　　whole number data type, one with no fraction part; a real number can have a fraction part. It's much harder for a computer to store and process real numbers than integers, so systems based on integer arithmetic can be cheap and fast.

internal sort　　sorting process working on a file held wholly in the main store (rather than in backing store).

interpreter　　machine code program used to translate and carry out the instructions of a high level language program one by one as it needs. Interpreting rather than compiling allows interactive programming and doesn't produce object code. On the other hand, the interpreter must remain in store all the time the high level program runs.

IT　　standard shorthand for information technology, the use of modern methods of handling information for the good of users and of society as a whole. Here "handling" information includes its capture, transfer, storage, access and processing, while the information may be as text, pictures, sound, or numbers.

There are various views of IT. All, however, welcome the convergence of once un-related technologies, eg, micro-electronics, video, computing and library science (information science).

item　　same as data structure or data item, an individual piece of information within an IT system.

iteration　　repeating a set (loop) of algorithm steps, strictly with the output value of one loop being the input to the next. Thus the value sought is refined. This process goes on (as set by the calling program) until either the value's within the required range or its size changes no longer. Iteration is the basis of many algorithms for the solution of mathematical (and thus scientific and engineering) problems.

key   data item which identifies a set of related data items. In most cases the set of data items makes up a record in a file, and the key value is in the key field. If the file's key field values aren't unique, there may be a need for a secondary key in a second field. In not all files is the key field always the same − if users search a file for different types of data the key may well change.

key word   one of the set of strings a program language translator will recognise and translate − such as REPEAT, TO, ELSE. In some languages key words are reserved − programmers can't use them as labels in programs, or, sometimes, even include them within labels (as with sTOpvalue).

label   the name given to a program or block, or, in one, to a constant, variable quantity, instruction or procedure. It's easier for the programmer to refer to any of these by name than by value or by storage address: the translation program takes care of the details, including by building up and referring to a label table.

language   system (set of rules and structures) for expressing ideas in spoken or symbol form. All human languages (natural languages) are very rich and complex, having developed over thousands of years in most cases. The languages used to give instructions to IT systems (see program languages) are far simpler − with far smaller vocabularies (sets of key words) and far fewer and more rigid rules (the syntax, or grammar).

A language translator is a program that takes in statements in one language and converts them to statements in another. While there are more and more effective programs for translating text between pairs of human languages, the phrase mainly refers to the programs (assembler, compiler, interpreter) that translate program instructions to machine code.

library   set of functions or routines (or procedures) a programmer finds often worth drawing from (rather than trying to design from scratch each time).

life cycle   the series of steps and actions between recognising that a problem exists in a system and having a chosen solution in place and fully working – the essence of systems analysis. The mains steps are:

- systems analysis as such, and feasibility study
- choice of solution
- design of solution
- implementation (which includes testing and staff training).

The process tends to be cyclic in that, after some time, the new system will show new problems as work load grows or circumstances change.

linear   logically in one dimension only. Thus a linear program (or program section) has no branches, and therefore no loops or other structures that involve decision.

link   same as pointer, in the case of pointers between the logically adjacent members of a linked list or ring data structure. A linked list is a logically linear (one dimensional) structure to which you can add, and from which you can remove, data items (elements) at any point. There's a pointer (link) to the head of the list in the system's label table; the head carries a pointer to the next item, and so on to the tail (the last item). Some linked lists allow each element to carry a second pointer, the address of the item before it in the list. Amending the list in either case is simply a question of changing the pointers. A linked ring is a linked list whose tail points to the head.

list   series of data items or structures (eg strings, file records), list processing (eg with the language Lisp) being the processing of data in the form of linked lists. A linked list (or chain) is a linear data structure into which you can insert, and from which you can remove, items (elements) at any point – see link.

local   nearby. To a programmer, a local variable is a variable with a label recognised only in one part

	(procedure) of a program; a global variable plays a part throughout the program's procedures.
location	a single storage cell, with its own address, in main or backing store.
logarithmic search	same as binary search (binary chop).
logical	related to some aspect of logic. A logical type in programming is a data item with no more than two values, called, for instance, 0 and 1, true and false, or no and yes. In the instruction IF flag THEN ..., flag is a logical with only two possible values (set or not set).
loop	set of instructions in a program the IT system may pass through a number of times. There are three kinds of loop algorithm; in Basic the structures are – DOTHIS/.../TIMES n, where n is a number – for when the programmer knows how many times the system should pass through the loop instructions – REPEAT/.../UNTIL ... – for when the system must pass through the loop instructions at least once, until the stated condition becomes true – WHILE .../.../ENDWHILE – much the same, except this time, if the condition is true, the system doesn't pass through the loop at all.
low level	close to the way an IT system works rather than to the way a human thinks (high level), a low level program language being one the system can follow without further translation (ie machine code).
machine	in the context of IT, any single stand alone unit or system, in particular a computer (whether special purpose or general purpose). A machine – ie computer – is a complex of electronic circuits designed to carry out some range of tasks under the control of one or more programs. Those programs must be in machine code – with all instructions as sets of bits (0s and 1s) the system can accept.
maintenance	keeping things working. In IT this applies not just to hardware (in the normal sense), but to software – keeping files current and backed up, and keeping programs up to date with changes in the users' needs. The latter is the main task of a maintenance programmer.

master

the file in current use for searching and sorting etc. At the same time as it's in use, new transactions make it more and more out of date. Every so often (in some cases once or twice a minute, more often daily) the master and transaction files are merged to produce a new master.

menu

list of options on display as offered by a program; the users make their choices by moving the cursor or pressing keys. As, at many stages in many interactive programs, there's a number of options, a menu's a good way to make the options clear. Menu-driven programs are more friendly than command-driven ones, but slower in action. Often, therefore, a program will try to combine both in such a way as to appeal to naive and expert users alike.

merging

process of linking parts, or the whole, of two files. A major task of file maintenance in a large system involves merging the current master file with the latest transaction file (which the program must first sort into the same sequence as the master). The process produces a new master for the users to work with (and an error report showing on which transactions merging failed). People call the old master the parent of the new one – the child.

module

chunk of a program that relates to a major single part of the outline algorithm, so has a major but single function. A module stands alone to a fair degree, so can be coded independently of other parts of the program, only being linked to, and tested in, the whole at a later stage. It's sometimes possible to set up module libraries, though this is more common with the somewhat smaller procedures.

Modular programming involves viewing a program as a set of modules, to allow ease of coding, testing, and maintenance.

numeric

concerned with number values, whether denary (decimal) or binary. A numeric (data type) has a purely numeric value, being, for instance, an integer, real, or complex number.

operating software/   the program or suite that controls all the resources
system (OS) of, processes in, and detailed action of a processor
in an IT system. There are many kinds of OS, each
machine needing its own several types for the
several types of usage (eg batch, multi-user,
parallel).

operator person with a role in looking after a large computer
system (where there's often a need for several in
each shift).

output data passed from a program or system to the user
or to a second program or system. An output
device/unit is an item of hardware designed to
produce or present output (eg microform, plotter,
printer, robot device, screen, speaker, video tape or
disk recorder).

package set of working computer software and manuals
(documentation) ready for distribution.

parallel in IT, working in step at the same time. In a parallel
computer, the operating software allocates tasks to
the many slave micro-processors for them to carry
out at the same time.

Parallel running often forms part of the
implementation stage of a system life cycle: a new
system is in place, and to check it (as well as to cope
if it breaks down), the staff run it in parallel with
the old system. In other words, all inputs pass to
the two systems, and the staff can compare the
outputs. This is more costly than the more usual
pilot running.

parameter a value (or label) passed between a procedure
(closed sub-routine) and its calling routine, or the
other way.

physical structure the actual layout of a file, for instance, in a store –
eg in blocks rather than in records (that being an
aspect of logical structure). It's for the operating and
applications software to take account of the physical
structure of stored data – the user may not even
need to know about the logical structure and, for
sure, should not find the user interface changed if
the physical structure changes.

pilot on trial or under test, pilot running being the testing of a newly installed system by using it with a small set of sample inputs – compare parallel running.

pointer address of a given data item stored so as to "point" to the location of that item. Thus the index of a file is a list of data item labels and pointers, as is a label table. Some data structures – eg linked list and tree – have pointers attached to each data item to link it to parent and child(ren).

procedure part of a program, viewed as a whole as handling a particular task within the overall algorithm, and kept separate from the main program. The main program, or a second procedure, calls on the procedure as required; at its end, control returns to the calling point.

program set of instructions in suitable form, so that, when translated, an IT system can carry them out to complete a given task. See also algorithm.

A program language is an environment for making programs – a set of rules and key words designed for tasks within a range of applications. The early programmers had to work in machine code – their programs were strings of 0s and 1s the computer could act upon directly. To make coding simpler for the people involved, assemblers, and then high level program languages appeared. For program structure, see algorithm and structure.

pseudocode method of writing algorithms – it looks like real code in that it uses many real structures and key words, but it isn't code any given translation software can handle (yet).

real (number) zero, or any positive or negative number which may include a fraction part as well as an integer part. The integers are a sub-set of the class of reals, but the ways IT systems tend to treat them differ.

record data structure which contains a number of fields, spaces (with labels) for related data items not all the same type (compare array), or a chunk of data treated by a system as a unit – ie, a physical record or block.

recursion   passing again and again through the same sub-routine (set of program actions) because the sub-routine calls itself.

searching   the reason for storing data, eg in a data base. In a large file there may be many thousand records. Methods of finding the right one(s) to meet a given need must be fast and effective – and easy to use; various approaches have come about in an attempt to make this possible.

sort   put the elements of a set into groups or into order (sequence) following some rule. Sorting is a major aspect of data processing, whether applied to a set of single data items or to lengthy records with a large number of fields in a file. For instance, a computer must sort the records of a transaction file into the same order as the master file before merging the two to make a new (up-to-date) master. Again, it's easier to search a file if it's sorted, and easier to compare the contents of two files sorted the same way.

source   origin, as in source code – a program in a high level language before translation into the machine code the system can follow.

statement   single complete meaningful scene-setting observation or instruction in a high level program language – or the symbols (code) in which the programmer may express it. Program languages differ somewhat in how they define the concept and what they may expect in terms of labels and separators.

static   not to change during an action or set of actions (eg, during a program run). Thus static data is the same as constant data (eg, the value of PI or the name of a firm as it may appear at the top of different screens and printouts).

stepwise   step by planned step, a way to describe programming techniques such as modular or top-down development.

string   set of any number of keyboard (or, for instance, ASCII) characters that a system can treat as a whole as regards storage, transfer and processing.

structure overall design of an algorithm and the program that develops from it. A structure chart shows program structure in graphic form – it's hierarchical, with each level giving more detail than the one above. Moreover, if you traverse ("walk round") the chart clockwise from the root, visiting each box on the way, you have a pseudocode version of the program. This allows you to produce structured code, at least if working with a structured program language.

This approach of devising a more and more detailed structure diagram for the algorithm, then converting it to pseudocode and final code, is a top-down approach to structured programming. Any approach to structured programming should much reduce the number of errors, and thus produce bug-free and efficient code with a minimum of effort.

sub-routine part of a longer program with a specific task within that program. A sub-routine may be open – lying within the main program itself – or closed – stored separately and called by the main program or by another sub-routine. The closed sub-routine is of more value to the programmer, especially when it's likely the program will need to use the sub-routine more than once.

subscript the label (index) of an element (data item) in a data structure. Thus "matrix(4,3)" could refer to the third element in the fourth row of the array called matrix – 4 and 3 are the element's subscripts.

system any combination of hardware, software, links, procedures and actions that help people carry out a task. In particular, an IT system is such a combination whose concern is the efficient handling of information.

The science (art?) of systems analysis involves taking a highly professional and expert view of existing systems (whether IT-based or not); the aim is not always to computerise – but it is always to attempt to define and design a better system for the purpose. However, the word "better" is not always easy to work with. The tasks of a systems analyst range right throughout system design, though on a large project different people will specialise in different areas.

table set of data set out logically in two or more dimensions with columns and rows (and pages, etc). An IT system's operating software uses a label table (look-up table) to hold the labels (names) of variable data items.

top down development/ programming approach to program development and coding which builds up more and more detail on an initial outline. The programmer breaks the starting concept into a set of stages, and repeats this process until able to code each stage as a program procedure or module.

trace to follow the action of a program through in a structured way, so the programmer can detect errors in program control (logic errors). This may be done by working through a dry run – in which the programmer takes input data sets in turn and passes manually through the program listing. On the other hand, many program languages provide some kind of trace utility to show on screen or paper which steps the run goes through. In either case, a trace table is of value. This shows how the values of variable data items change during a run.

transaction a single individual action or event that relates to the content of a file or data base, ie, one that requires the up-dating of a record. In the case of a stock file, transactions would include details of sales and deliveries, changes of some aspect of a product, new products, and products no longer on offer. During each trading period, a firm will build up a transaction file; every so often, the system will sort this and merge it with the master file to produce a new master.

tree set of one or more nodes (junctions), with a root node, and then one or more sub-trees. Trees appear in a number of contexts in IT theory, and not just to show hierarchical relationships and data structures as such.

utility program – usually small – designed to carry out a single routine task. Common utility programs (utility software) are print dumps, editors for assembly code, and error-handling routines.

variable   data item whose value is likely to change during a program run, or each time the program concerned runs. Because the programmer cannot, therefore, predict what the data item's value will be, it must be coded in a special way. In fact, it receives a label which, to the operating software's label table, refers to a given storage cell.

Appendix 2

References

Barnes J G P, *Programming in Ada*, 3rd ed, Addison Wesley, 1989

COBOL 85 Reference Summary, NCC, 1988

Davis W S, *Structured Systems Analysis and Design*, Addison Wesley, 1983

Elbra R A, *Database for the Small Computer User*, NCC, 1982

French C S, *Data Processing and Information Technology*, DP Publications 1990

Gray M, London K, *Documentation Standards*, Business Books, 1970

IT Starts Developers Guide, Crown Copyright, 1989

Martin J, McClure C, *Software Maintenance – The Problem and Its Solutions*, Prentice Hall, 1983

Prince: Structured Project Management Introductions, NCC Blackwell, 1990.

SSADM Training Student Notes, NCC, 1988

Student Notes on NCC Data Processing Documentation Standards, NCC, 1978

Appendix 3
Solutions to exercises

Chapter 1

Exercise One

a) HOUSE-NUMBER ← 257;

b) COUNTRY ← "England";

c) DAY ← 01;
MONTH ← "July";
YEAR ← 1991;

d) NUMBER ← NUMBER-3;

e) PERCENTAGE ← PERCENTAGE/2;

Exercise Two

a) input DAY-OF-WEEK, WEEK-NUMBER;

b) display NAME, BIRTHPLACE;

c) print SUBJECT, EXAM-MARK;

Exercise Three

a) Three numeric variables are required, for example NUMBER-1, NUMBER-2 and PERCENT, and the code (at its simplest) would be:

accept NUMBER-1, NUMBER-2
PERCENT ← 100/(NUMBER-1/NUMBER-2);

Checks can be added to work out which number is biggest, or a message added to request the numbers to be input in a certain order, eg the biggest first.

b) This could be the code:

```
display "Enter temperature in Fahrenheit";
accept FAHRENHEIT;
CENTIGRADE ← ((FAHRENHEIT–32)/9)*5;
display FAHRENHEIT, "degsF=", CENTIGRADE, "degsC";
```

The inclusion of suitable comments would improve the quality of the code.

NOTE: Exact punctuation is not all that important in pseudocode, but will be when it is translated into the computer language proper.

Exercise Four

```
display prompt;
accept EXAM-MARK;
if EXAM-MARK > = 70
   then GRADE ←1;
   else if EXAM-MARK > = 50
      then GRADE ←2;
      else if EXAM-MARK > = 40
            then GRADE ←3;
            else GRADE ←4;
            endif;
         endif;
   endif;
display EXAM-MARK,GRADE;
```

Chapter 2

Exercise One

a)   fixed point number, variable, character string, integer, expression, floating point number

b)   (1) 22;   (2) FALSE;   (3) John is older;   (4) TRUE;   (5) TRUE

Exercise Two

1)

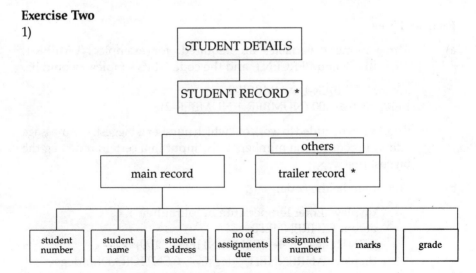

2 a) Although there can only be (as far as we know) either no phone number, or a single phone number, this can either be a REPETITION construct or a SELECTION depending on the action that we take. If we do something different when there is no phone number from what we do if there is a phone number then it should be a SELECTION, otherwise it should be a REPETITION.

Assuming the former: the latter:

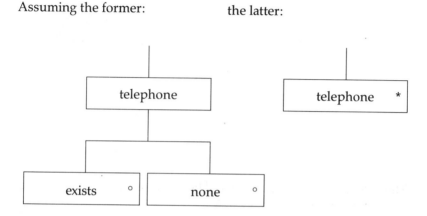

b) This is a SELECTION, either initials or first name, so we need to put an "O" in the INITIALS rectangle and add a rectangle with FIRSTNAME and "O" in it. However, the rules are that *all* the boxes connected to another box have to be SELECTION if one is, so we have to put a dummy box in to cover it, thus:

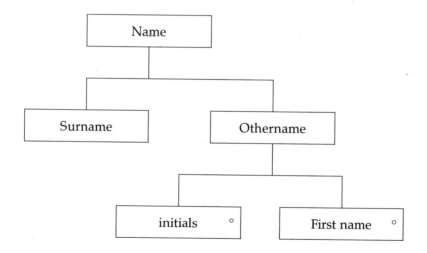

Exercise Three

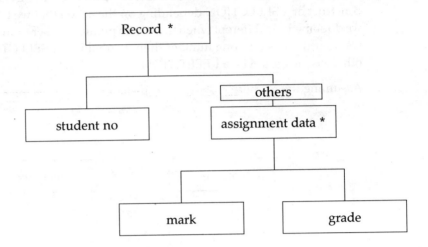

The field assignment details would be represented by a subscripted variable with an index varying from 1 to 6.

Chapter 3

Exercise One

C = 0
A = 2
R = 1

Table 1	1
read stock	X
read used-on	X
goto TABLE 2	x

C = 2
A = 2
R = 3

Table 2	1	2	3
end of stockfile?	Y	N	N
end of used-on?	-	Y	N
goto TABLE 3	-	-	x
Close files : END	X	X	

C = 3
A = 9
R = 4

Table 3	1	2	3	4
stock < used-on?	Y	Y	N	N
stock > used-on?	-	-	Y	N
'development' part?	Y	N	-	-
WARNING — part not used	-	X	-	-
read stock	X	X	-	-
ERROR — files out of step	-	-	X	-
Close files : END	-	-	X	-
Calc. part requirement	-	-	-	X
establish stock & order form	-	-	-	X
output demand pattern	-	-	-	X
goto TABLE 1	-	-	-	X
goto TABLE 2	X	X	-	-

Notes on Decision Tables:

1. Any limited entry decision table (condition entries shown by Y, N or − only) has a precise number of rules or implied rules. With N conditions, there will be 2^N rules; one condition, 2 rules; 2 conditions, 4 rules and so on. To check this, look at TABLE 2. There are 2 conditions, so there should be 4 rules or implied rules. Each "−" means "both Y and N", so Rule 1 actually contains 2 implied rules. If a rule has three "−" signs, it has 2^3 (=8) implied rules.

2. If there are no conditions, there are 2^0 rules − or if your mathematics went that far − 1 rule. 'Anything' to the power of "zero" equals 1. This is convenient for showing any initial actions before any decisions, in a set of decision tables − TABLE 1 illustrates a zero condition table. If "end of file" were a programmed test (say for a known high value), then the fourth action in TABLE 3 could be replaced by "set high-value", and rule 3 would have an additional "X" in the ninth action − goto TABLE 2.

3. To allow comparison with the flow chart, the tables have been produced in a similar sequence. If a decision table pre-processor or processor was used, then the resulting code would not be as efficient as it could be. In TABLE 3, for example, the most efficient code would probably be produced by making condition 1, "stocked=used-on?", and putting the rules in the sequence 4,3,1,2,. The most frequently found result of the tests would then be the first rule, and much unnecessary testing would be saved.

Chapter 4

Exercise One

This is a suggested solution containing the barest elements, there will be others which are just as acceptable.

```
while not QUIT
   do
      display INTRO-SCREEN;
      accept CODE-NUMBER;
      if CODE-NUMBER-NOT-OK
         then
            display ERROR-MESSAGE;
         else
            perform BILLING;

      endif;

   endo;
```

VALIDATION ROUTINE

SYSTEM CONTROL OF PROCEDURE TO ENSURE REPETITIVE LOOP

Exercise Two

Points needing clarification in the program specification

Note that you will not be asked to actually code any part of this work, so that actual details of file and record layouts are irrelevant. However, viewed as a program specification, the following points would be relevant.

1.

Ref2   Stock File Main Record. Insufficient detail of sequence of the file (it is sequential, in ascending order of Part Number). Insufficient detail of record and file layout, medium on which stored, item sizes and types.

2.   Stock File Trailer Record. As for main record – also it is necessary to know how to identify a trailer record (different record type), and how many are on file. Average and maximum values should be provided. (Average 1 per part on file, maximum known historically is 3 for a part.)

3.   Product Breakdown. More details of field sizes, etc needed (see "Note" at the top).

4.   Used-on file. As above.

5.1   What number of products should be allowed for? It is insufficient to say "there may be more than 20". (Allow 25.) Does the program insist on receiving all 10 weeks' data, or should it be possible to input forecasts for shorter periods, or specific weeks only?

(Since all stock may be used up in the early weeks of a forecast, current week must be input – and no week can be "skipped over". However, a forecast may be terminated after any number of weeks, if desirable.)

5.2 Is it possible to feed known delays to receipt of orders into the system, and thus to give a more realistic due date?

(Yes, the normal lead time could be increased, but that is the only way. Order dates cannot be altered.)

5.3 "Printed or Displayed". Is this a programmer decision, a user decision at run-time, or what? (For the forecasting element of the task, the user requires display, with option of printout if required at the time of the run, after seeing the display for a part. The printout would be for the specific part just displayed. Alternatively, the user could indicate "full print required" at the program start, and the display would be suppressed.)

General

What "week numbering" system is used?

The existing system to maintain the stock file is mentioned, but should be described, or the structure should be indicated (updated daily, weekly, or when.) No programming language or hardware details are supplied – although the specification appears to assume that the work will be done by an external programmer, not an existing employee. The source of the data for the Product Breakdown file is not supplied – nor is file set-up mentioned.

Since the program for which this is a specification reads the "Used-on" file, presumably its format and content is known. It is not provided.

Chapter 5

Exercise One

a) Some others that might be mentioned are:

understandability	how easy or difficult it is to understand a particular program
reliability	the program performing as expected, consistently
testability	how easy the program is to test effectively
modifiability	how successfully the program can be modified
usability	how easy the programs are for the user to use
portability	the program is easily transferrable to other systems
efficiency	the way the program uses resources

Here are some examples of good practices:

b)

Understandability	good structuring
	comment blocks for each module, subroutine, etc
	consistent layout
	brackets used to clarify the evaluation order in arithmetic statements

Reliability	input data validated before use
	tests exercise most of the execution paths
	subscript ranges are tested before being used
	checks included for potentially catastrophic arithmetic operations, eg divide by zero

Testability	good modularisation and structuring
	descriptive error messages
	tracing and displaying of logical flow optional
	compexity minimised

Modifiability	variables used in preference to constants
	good documentation kept up-to-date, standard library routines used for common functions
	variables used logically whenever possible

Usability	help feature included
	adequate, non-threatening error messages abbreviated commands for experienced users
	no specialised DP knowledge required

Portability	high-level machine-independent language
	minimal use of operating systems functions
	standard language features and library subroutines
	machine dependent statements isolated and documented

Efficiency	exception routines and error handling in separate modules
	optimising compiler use
	mixed data types in arithmetic operations avoided
	likeliest TRUE expression tested first in complex conditions

These are just a sample, many more can be found.

Chapter 6

Exercise One

a) Black box (or functional) testing and white-box (or structural) testing

b) Possible, probable and absolute correctness

Absolute correctness can only be achieved by testing all the possible combinations for input values; this cannot be done in an acceptable amount of time. Also even if it were, some code would not be tested, therefore all the paths in the code have to be checked as well; again there are so many as to make this impractical.

Chapter 7

Exercise One

a) (1) parallel running
   (2) full change-over or "sudden death"
   (3) pilot installation
   (4) phased installation

b) (1) advantages: old system continues to run alongside the new one, therefore if the new system has faults, no live data is affected

   disadvantages: extra effort is needed to run both systems and compare results

   (2) advantages: quickly implemented

   disadvantages: if testing has not been thorough enough, and errors occur, the live data will be affected

   (3) advantages: the option is open to cancel if the implementation is unsuccessful; errors can be corrected before the whole user-base is implemented

   disadvantages: takes time to implement; needs extra effort for co-ordination

| (4) | advantages | basic or most-wanted features can be implemented quickly; the output from each stage can be fully checked before the next is begun |
| | disadvantages: | takes time to implement fully; some errors may only be found late in the installation, but which may affect already implemented parts of the system. |

Chapter 8

Exercise One

a) Inital study
System design
Program design
Coding
Testing
Installation
Live running
Review

b) The one basic criticism of this model is that it does not accurately reflect reality. It covers the stages of system development as if they were a flow of steps one after another, each one being completed before the next one is begun. This is not the case in the real world. Change is inevitable and continually affects the development of computer systems. Before each stage ends there will be requests for alterations, and some changes will affect stages that have already been completed. To produce an accurate model some means of representing this would have to be included.

Chapter 9

Exercise One

The four essential features are:

- data description
- data manipulation
- data communication
- sequence control.

Exercise Two

The print program! Surprised? Well, this is why. If the print program is given priority the number of transfers is so high that very little CPU attention would be required. The print program would proceed as if it were the only one in the system, whilst the main file update would be executed during the "wait" states in almost the same time as if it were running alone. If done the other way round, the system would give very little time to the print program, hence the total time would be the same as if the two programs were run one after the other.

Chapter 10

Exercise One

Some examples are (not in order of importance):

1) file handling (so I wouldn't have to leave the program to load and save files)

2) full-screen editing (so I could see the code I was working with easily)

3) line-by-line interpreter (to check the code for syntactic correctness before compiling it, so errors would be easier to associate with specific lines)

4) built-in compiler links (so I wouldn't have to quit to compile)

5) symbolic debugger (to see the values in important variables change as the program executes line-by-line)

6) on-screen output design (so I could design a screen or printout, then have this translated automatically into source code).

Appendix 4

Sample exam paper

> **CANDIDATES MUST ATTEMPT THIS QUESTION**
> **ALL PARTS ARE EQUALLY WEIGHTED (2 MARKS EACH)**

QUESTION 1

a) Give an example of the SELECTION construct in programming.

b) Give an appropriate DATA TYPE for each of the following DATA ITEMS:

   i) A person's age in years.

   ii) A bank balance.

c) From the following DATA STRUCTURE DIAGRAM give two different possible values for such a DATA ITEM.

NAME

TITLE	INITIAL *		LAST NAME		
Mr.°------Ms°	A° B° --- Z°		SMITH°	JONES°	BROWN°

d) A program is designed using STEPWISE REFINEMENT. How does this affect when testing may take place?

e) How can a programmer's choice of IDENTIFIERS improve program coding?

f) Give two possible outputs from a COMPILER.

g) What is the importance of PROGRAM LANGUAGE LIBRARIES to a programmer?

h) How, other than by the program code, can the DESIGN of a program be DOCUMENTED?

i) State the difference between a SYNTAX ERROR and a LOGICAL (SEMANTIC) ERROR in a program.

j) State one way in which the use of an APPLICATION PROGRAM GENERATOR may reduce coding time.

k) A PROGRAM SPECIFICATION is the first formal request for a new program. Give two items which it should contain.

l) How can PROGRAM MAINTENANCE be made easier by adopting an INSTALLATION STANDARD?

THIS QUESTION MUST BE ATTEMPTED

QUESTION 2

PROGRAM CODING should be used to illustrate the answers to this question and you should state which language you are using with each example.

RECORDS in a DATA FILE contain the following four DATA ITEMS:
    A DEVICE CODE of the form "ddcu", for example — DUA7.
    The dd represents the device type of which there are three, DU, DJ, DR.
    The c is the type of controller (possible values A — Z).
    The u is the unit number range with possible values 0 — 9.

A DEVICE DESCRIPTION of up to 30 characters.

A STORAGE CAPACITY measured in MEGABYTES with a maximum of 999 MB.

A DATE OF LAST OVERHAUL.

The records will, consequently, appear as, for example:-

| DUA0 | Fixed RA81 Disk | 456 | 24/04/89 |
| DJB2 | Removable RA60 Disk | 205 | 17/02/89 |

a) Design an appropriate FILE STRUCTURE which will allow access to any significant part of any DATA ITEM in any RECORD.

b) Using your FILE STRUCTURE from a) follow the appropriate PROGRAM DEVELOPMENT STAGES to produce CODE to PROCESS ALL RECORDS from the file to produce separate OUTPUT FILES for each of the following REPORTS:-

   i) The total STORAGE CAPACITY, for all records, for each type of device, eg a total for all type DU, a total for all DJ, etc.

   ii) A list of DEVICE CODES for all devices not overhauled within the last three months.

Marks will be awarded as follows:-

File structure	6 marks
Good design technique	6 marks

Correct use of PROGRAM STRUCTURE   7 marks
For each of the two OUTPUT FILE DESIGNS   3 marks
   For following GOOD CODING PRACTICE   3 marks

CANDIDATE MUST <u>NOT</u> ATTEMPT MORE THAN
THREE FURTHER QUESTIONS

QUESTION 3

a)   Explain, with examples, each of the two program constructs SEQUENCE and ITERATION.

b)   Describe clearly the rules for carrying out ARITHMETIC OPERATIONS in a HIGH LEVEL LANGUAGE with which you are familiar.

c)   Give an example of a PRE-DEFINED FUNCTION in a programming language.

QUESTION 4

a)   Explain the difference between PROGRAM SPECIFICATION and PROGRAM DOCUMENTATION.

b)   Program documentation usually includes a USER GUIDE and a MAINTENANCE PROGRAMMER'S REFERENCE SECTION. For EACH of these identify TWO elements which you would expect to find and explain why each of the four items which you have chosen is needed in that particular part of the documentation.

QUESTION 5

A PROGRAMMER, having designed a program, will then CODE it.
Explain:-

a)   How the programmer will enter code into the machine.

b)   How the programmer will produce a program which will run.

c)   How any errors in the code will be likely to be found.

d)   How a BATCH JOB may be used for a TEST RUN.

QUESTION 6

The TESTING of a program may be OFF-LINE (sometimes called DESK-TOP testing), or ON-LINE.

a)   Explain, as clearly as you can, BOTH:-

    i)   ON-LINE testing and
    ii)   OFF-LINE testing.

b)   A program routine is to VALIDATE a date of birth. Explain what data you would use to test that routine.

c)   Give an example of the use of DUMMY STUBS in program testing.

QUESTION 7

A programmer must be aware of alternative methods of producing software using packages such as DATABASE MANAGEMENT and SPREADSHEET systems.

EITHER:-

By reference to a DATABASE MANAGEMENT SYSTEM with which you are familiar:-

a)   Describe three common INTERACTIVE COMMANDS available in the package.

b)   Explain how a programmer may use:-

    i)   VARIABLES
    ii)   SUBROUTINES
    iii)   INPUT and OUTPUT SCREEN FORMATS
        to create application software.

OR:-

From your experience of a SPREADSHEET SYSTEM, which you should identify:-

c)   Describe how it may be used to see the effects of varying the contents of a cell or cells in a "WHAT IF" situation.

d)   Describe how the programmer may use:-

    i)   FUNCTIONS
    ii)   MACROS
        to create application software.

Appendix 5

Mark scheme for sample exam paper

QUESTION 1

a) Can be either code, pseudocode or flowchart format:
If statement or decision box is OK, but better is conditional expression and statement (code) or decision box with "Y" and "N" alternatives (flowchart).

b) NUMERIC would be OK, but better (i)=INTEGER and (ii) REAL or FLOATING POINT

c) Using a combination from:

		SMITH	
M R	A	or	
o r	to	JONES	would be OK
M S	Z	or	
		BROWN	

but better if the two examples have a <u>different number</u> of initials – INITIAL is an iteration.

d) Program parts can be tested separately and testing can take place throughout the development stages.

e) Easier to read is OK, but better to add that the name can also be used to imply the type of contents.

f)   object code
       error listing
       source code listing
       cross reference mapping

g) To save time is enough, but adding that code can be shared thus avoiding duplication of work and increasing reliability, is better.

h) Flowchart is OK, but better to imply structured approach,

   i e structure chart
        decision table
        pseudocode
        Jackson structure diagram
        Nassi-Shneiderman chart.

i) syntax = incorrect spelling or grammer of language logic or semantic = incorrect processing of data.

j) Standard types of operations such as sorts, searches and validation can be generated without the need for the programmer to develop special code.

k) input specification
    output specification
    processing requirements
    scope/limitations

l) If everyone sticks to a standard then everyone will understand each other's work. Examples are:-

    naming conventions
    methods for standard operations
    layout of code etc.

QUESTION 2

The answer should contain the following (COBOL and BASIC are used as example languages.)

File structure

COBOL

Filename
Separate record name
At least 2 separate fields
All four fields identified
Reasonable data types
Parts of data field separately identified

BASIC

Filename present
Single variable name
Evidence of string manupulation in the code to access the above

Design Techniques

1) There should be more than one level of program design.

2) Within the code there should be the correct use of program blocks, eg paragraphs, procedures, subroutines, etc, within clearly defined Initialisation and Termination procedures.

Program Constructs

1) There should be a looping mechanism to process all records, containing:

> correct initialisation
> record reading
> termination procedures.

2) If statement to produce records for the output file.

3) A cumulative totalling mechanism for the output file.

Output File Design

A reasonable output record layout for each file, with headings, is needed.

Coding Practice

> Meaningful data names
> Use of indentation in layout
> Comments

QUESTION 3

a) Sequence
Explain the meaning, ie a group of statements executed one after another, and illustrate it with an example.

Iteration
It is important to bring out the concept of a loop, and provide an example. If more than one type of loop is described and another example given, this is better, eg FOR and WHILE loops.

b) An example of the simplest form: variable = expression, eg a = 2*3, is needed; additionally using more than one operator, using brackets and explaining the rules of precedence would be good.

c) Showing the form of a functional call, and explaining what it does is required; supplying other information about the use of parameters, and incorporating the function call in an expression, or assignment, is better still.

QUESTION 4

a) A program specification is a request for a program to be written; it is a ''prescriptive'' document, ie it says what should be done, and contains:

> input spec
> output spec
> processing requirements
> scope and limitations.

Program documentation is "descriptive", ie it contains a description of what exists, namely:

> data specifications
> logic description
> listings
> test plan
> user guide.
> maintenance guide.

b)   User guide contents:

> input description/requirements of program
> output description
> scope and range of data
> limitations
> operating instructions
> hardware requirements.

Maintenance guide contents:

> program specification
> design description
> program code listing
> glossary of variables
> testing runs and test data description.

Pick two from each and explain the aim/purpose of including them.

QUESTION 5

Either:

a)   Use an editor or word processor (explain what it does); or use a data preparation department + coding sheets; or use an interpreter/editor as on a home computer.

Either:

b)   Mention compiler, explain process in what comes out, then explain linking; or
explain RUN command in interactive, interpreted BASIC.

c)   <u>syntax</u> errors will be detected by the interpreter/compiler
<u>run-time</u> errors will be detected by the operating system or interpreter
<u>logical</u> errors will be found during inspection and dry-runs and testing of the code in an on-line environment.

d)   The batch method involves running a program from a file of job control, or operating system commands; there is no facility for interactive intervention or recovery.

QUESTION 6

a)   i)   On-line testing involves running the program using specially selected data. This data is chosen for specific reasons, eg to test whether the program can handle large volumes of data and the results of the run can be monitored using de-bugging code.

     ii)   Off-line testing comprises dry-running and desk-checking of code. The data chosen must represent the exceptional, ie zero values, extremes of ranges, etc as it is a time-consuming activity.

b)   Chosen values must be inside and outside the ranges normally considered for valid data, eg 33 of month 13. Also zero and negative values need to be tested.

c)   Dummy stubs are used for procedures which will be coded after testing, either because the testing is concerned with a higher level in the program structure, ie top-down approach, or because the module has not yet been written.

QUESTION 7

a)   Examples might be: (from ORACLE)

     i)   SELECT – to select any record from a table given some predefined criterion

        eg SELECT * FROM Product
           WHERE Product No = 2147

     ii)   JOIN – to join two tables and produce a third

        eg SELECT * FROM Order-Lines, Product
                 WHERE Order-Lines. Product No =
                           Product.Product No
               AND Description = 'Bott';

     iii)   CREATE – to create table

        eg CREATE TABLE Product
           (. . all the parameters . . .);

b)   i)   these can be used to for example contain user input or a count loop value

     ii)   utility subprogram examples should be given

     iii)   use of format files to hold formats which can be "painted" using the package and stored, for example report format files.

c)   Using a formula as cell contents is a good example, changing the cells used and their contents, (with a suitable example).

d) Explanation of the use of functions with cell contents, plus examples

eg SUM $(I_1 \, . \, . \, I_{10})$

e) Macros should emphasise the economy of use eg keystroke store, and the use for specialist functions such as IF( ) and control of execution of macro structure.

Index